The Role of
Strategy Statements

CPMR Research Report
2

The Role of
Strategy Statements

Richard Boyle
Síle Fleming

INSTITUTE OF PUBLIC
ADMINISTRATION

First published in 2000
by the Institute of Public Administration
57-61 Lansdowne Road
Dublin 4
Ireland
in association with
The Committee for Public Management Research

www.ipa.ie

British Library Cataloguing in Publication Data
A catalogue record for this book is available from the British
Library.

ISBN 1 902448 36 7
ISSN 1393-9424

Cover design by M & J Graphics Ltd
Typeset by the Institute of Public Administration
Printed by ColourBooks Ltd, Dublin

CONTENTS

Executive Summary

Under the terms of the Public Service Management Act, 1997, there is a statutory requirement on all government departments and offices to produce a strategy statement once every three years, or within six months of the appointment of a new minister. Strategy statements must set out the key objectives, outputs and related strategies (including the use of resources) of the department or office concerned. They are seen as a central element in the development of a strategic management process in the Irish civil service.

This report aims to review progress to date with the formulation and implementation of strategy statements. In particular, an assessment is made of the first two sets of strategy statements, published in 1996 and 1998. Lessons are drawn from this experience to guide future practice. The research framework established to facilitate the review focuses on three elements: (a) the content of strategy statements; (b) the process by which statements are derived and implemented; and (c) the impacts and linkages which strategy statements are intended to secure in practice.

The content of strategy statements
The study indicates significant improvements in the quality of statements overall from 1996 to 1998. The 1998 statements tend to cover a more diverse range of issues, and in greater depth, than the 1996 statements. However, significant limitations with many statements still exist, indicating scope for improvements in further iterations. Particular issues identified include:

- A weak link in some statements between environmental analysis and the objectives and strategies set out in the statement.
- Limited discussion of the resource implications of pursuing objectives, outputs and strategies, and some confusion with regard to understanding of these terms.
- Little evidence of assessment of customer/client needs.
- A tendency to list cross-departmental issues rather than set out what needs to be done and how in order to secure better co-ordination.

- Lack of clarity with regard to many of the performance measures used, and only a limited range of activities covered by performance measures.

- Insufficient attention in some cases to how the strategic management process is to be embedded into departmental practice.

Process issues associated with strategy statements
The content of strategy statements does not give a full picture of the state of strategic management in departments and offices. Indeed, an overemphasis on content runs the danger of neglecting significant issues. It is also necessary to focus on the process of formulating and subsequently implementing strategy.

With regard to strategy formulation, the study highlights the importance of involving staff in the formulation process, so as to encourage shared ownership. In practice, mechanisms employed by departments and offices range from those of a highly participative nature, in which staff are actively involved in formulating strategies, to more traditional top-down approaches, in which staff appear to have little input into the process.

The study also notes that developing the internal capacity required to secure strategy implementation may require changes to organisational culture. As a result, there is a need to adopt a planned approach to managing internal change, including changes to existing human resource systems and organisational structure. The findings suggest that the alignment of human resource systems and organisational structures with strategy is a challenging yet critical element of strategy implementation.

The impact and linkages arising from strategy statements
In general, there has been a positive response to the introduction of strategy statements. They are seen as contributing usefully to the running of departmental business. The fact that managers and staff have a more explicit statement of what it is they are trying to achieve is cited as a benefit. So too is the move to a more collective view by senior management of the direction of the department. The impact of strategy statements on relationships between senior civil servants and ministers

has been more limited, as have the impacts on staff generally.

The study shows the importance of developing linkages with other management processes, if strategy statements are to play a central role in the management of departments and offices. In particular, the need for strategy statements to inform and be informed by the business planning process is highlighted. It is through the business planning process that objectives and strategies are realised. Review and reporting mechanisms also have an important role to play in tracking progress, with the annual progress report providing a potentially useful means of reporting on performance. However, the first set of annual progress reports produced in 1999 fail in general to present a balanced picture, with little sense portrayed of problems encountered or targets not met.

The study also stresses the need to develop processes and procedures to deal with unplanned and unexpected events. The impact of strategy statements is limited if they become fossilised and departments and offices fail to identify or create means of responding to changing circumstances.

Recommendations to enhance the role of strategy statements
Finally, the report identifies aspects of practice which can be developed to improve strategy statements in the future.

Strategy statement formulation
- Strategy should be formulated to take account of the collective views of the organisation, in order to ensure greater ownership of the strategic management process. A range of mechanisms can be deployed to this end, including the use of cross-functional teams and task-based groups. At the same time, there is a need for the senior management team to provide direction and leadership to ensure that the statement retains an appropriate high-level strategic focus.

- The formulation of strategies requires a challenging appraisal of existing activities and a prioritisation of strategic choices, since not all strategies may be financially or operationally feasible within available resources. This implies the need for a realistic assessment of available resources within the context of desired objectives, and as a consequence a reallocation of financial and human resources to what are identified as the most strategically important concerns.

- With regard to the specific formulation of strategy statements, there are a number of issues which must be addressed. Ministers, and politicians more generally, need to be engaged with the process, given their key role in providing support for needed changes. Staff too must be meaningfully engaged in the formulation process. The partnership process provides a long-term and institutionalised means of engaging staff. It should be recognised that staff and management may need to be equipped with the necessary skills and competencies to engage in strategy formulation in a partnership or other collaborative forum. For example, specific skills and competencies may need to be developed to ensure that activities such as environmental analysis are properly carried out.

Strategy statement content
- Environmental analysis must clearly be seen to link through to the resulting objectives and strategies, with the implications of the analysis clearly specified. More use should be made of techniques such as scenario planning and open simulation to deal with uncertain futures. Also, the findings from programme reviews and evaluations need to feed into the environmental analysis.

- Goals, objectives and strategies need to be clearly defined and specified, with goals and objectives focused on outcomes where possible. Where achievement of goals and objectives is outside the direct control of a department or office, intermediate objectives should be set. The resource implications regarding the achievement of goals and objectives should be addressed in general terms, particularly in the context of multi-annual budgeting.

- Customer/client expectations and needs assessments should clearly be a major driver of issues covered in strategy statements (including internal customers). The linkages between the strategy statement and Customer Action Plans should be clear.

- In detailing cross-departmental issues and cross-functional linkages, statements should identify the issues of concern, outline who is involved and highlight what needs to be done. Actions needed to secure and improve co-operation and co-ordination should be detailed where possible.

- The specification of performance measures in statements is a challenging task, but one which requires further action. Having goals, objectives and strategies which are focused on results and are as specific as possible facilitates the development of performance measures. Measures need to be developed for as wide a range of activities as possible, including the development of measures from a customer/client perspective.

- Statements should describe and acknowledge the role played by staff in the development of strategy statements. They should also clearly set out the organisational implications arising from the embedding of the strategic management process. Structural and organisation development changes needed to ensure that strategies are achieved should be identified and actions should be proposed in these areas as necessary.

Strategy implementation
- To ensure the effective implementation of strategy, there is a need to devise human resource strategies to fit business strategy. Notwithstanding the range of influences which impact on human resource planning in the civil service (for example, centralised recruitment and selection, interdepartmental mobility through promotion) policies need to be developed in relation to promotion and training and development to ensure that the right competencies and resources are available to achieve business objectives.

- Strategy implementation implies change, and as a consequence, there is a need to plan and manage the change process effectively through the use of organisation development interventions such as partnership committees and team-based projects. As with any organisation development initiative, such interventions should be designed to challenge existing assumptions and patterns of behaviour in order to meaningfully engage staff in the achievement of cultural change, and as a consequence, strategy.

- Many strategies require co-operation with other agencies if they are to be implemented effectively. Tensions and issues of territoriality need to be addressed as part of the implementation process. Improved communications between policy makers and service deliverers is particularly important in securing effective delivery of cross-cutting strategies.

- There must be clear links between strategy statements and business plans. Equally, business plans should be translated to individual level if the strategy statement is to inform the day-to-day work of individuals. The introduction of performance management should provide a mechanism by which individual objectives can be formally identified and integrated with other performance-related issues, including training and development plans and performance measurement.

- Annual progress reports need to present a balanced picture of performance, highlighting both progress made and problems encountered. Also, in addition to formal reporting requirements under the Public Service Management Act, 1997, continuous mechanisms need to be put in place to provide for reporting of divisional and individual progress against desired objectives.

- There should be a better integration and synchronisation between strategy implementation and performance and financial management systems. For example, the evaluation of efficiency and effectiveness of strategies and goals through expenditure programme reviews should be used to inform subsequent strategy formulation. Similarly, multi-annual budgeting and accruals-based accounting have the potential to facilitate a more strategic outlook in financial terms. Departments and offices should also ensure that activities such as business planning, review and annual reports, performance management and the estimates process are synchronised and work together rather than be separate exercises which put a strain on resources.

It is important that strategy statements are seen as part of a *process* of strategic management. Statements on their own have limited value. They must be at the hub of a range of management activities including business planning, performance management, budgetary allocation and human resource strategy. But an emphasis on process alone is not enough. It is also important to emphasise *action*. Just as statements themselves are incomplete unless part of a wider strategic management process, similarly the process itself is only of limited value unless it leads to the desired actions.

PART 1

Introduction

1.1 Focus of report

This report on the role of strategy statements was carried out by the Committee for Public Management Research. The study focuses on the place of strategy statements in the management of government departments and offices. Through an analysis of the content of strategy statements and the process through which they are produced and implemented, the main elements needed to ensure effective strategy statements are identified. Good practice examples are highlighted. The importance of linking strategy statements to business planning and resource allocation is identified. The report concludes with a number of recommendations towards the future development of strategy statements.

1.2 Study background and terms of reference

Strategy statements are a central part of the government's Strategic Management Initiative (SMI). As a formal expression of the strategic management process in government departments and offices, strategy statements are intended to set out the key strategies and objectives to be achieved over a three year period. Under the Public Service Management Act, 1997, there is a statutory requirement on all government departments and offices to produce a strategy statement once every three years, or within six months of the appointment of a new minister.

As a relatively new initiative, strategy statements are still evolving. The intention is that they will encourage the adoption of a longer-term focus on strategic policy issues. But for the statements to operate effectively a number of questions need to be addressed. How are strategic priorities identified? To what extent should statements be drawn up in consultation with staff? How are unplanned and unexpected events dealt with? It is to address these and other related questions that the terms of reference for the study were determined. It was agreed that the study would aim to:

a) Analyse the content and role of strategy statements, based on official documentation and legislation and discussions with key officials, and assess existing statements against their defined role.

b) Undertake a thorough review of relevant national and international research evidence on the role of written agreements in facilitating the strategic management of public service organisations.

c) Review practice with regard to the role of strategy statements in the management of a cross section of government departments and offices, focusing in particular on the linkages between strategy statements and business planning.

d) Make recommendations as to the steps needed to ensure the effective use of strategy statements as a means of good strategic management practice in the Irish public service.

1.3 Study approach and methodology

The study commenced in April 1999 and was completed in December 1999. Three main sources of information were used in the study:

1. *Literature review.* The literature, both academic and from official government sources, was reviewed. This provided contextual material, plus information on the experience of other countries with strategic planning. The US in particular was found to have useful documentation on departmental strategic plans, arising from the Government Performance and Results Act, 1993.

2. *Content analysis of strategy statements.* Strategy statements for government departments and offices published in 1996 and 1998 were reviewed (see Annex 1 for a list of the strategy statements reviewed). These published statements provided insight into the practice

of strategy statement preparation and the content areas covered in statements.

3. *Selected key interviews.* In order to obtain more in-depth information on the process of strategy statement preparation and the statements' impact to date, interviews took place with selected senior managers from four government departments and offices: the Department of Enterprise, Trade and Employment; the Department of the Environment and Local Government; the Department of the Marine and Natural Resources; and the Office of the Revenue Commissioners. These organisations were chosen to give a mix of civil service departments in terms of size, staffing and diversity of activities. While not claiming to be representative of the civil service as a whole, the organisations chosen cover a broad range of civil service activities among them. They were also all among a range of departments and offices whose 1998 strategy statements illustrate examples of good practice in a number of areas.

1.4 Report structure

Part 2 sets out the formal role of strategy statements, based on official documentation and legislation. It also outlines a framework for the study, centred around three main concerns: the content of strategy statements; the process by which statements are derived and delivered; and the impact and linkages which strategy statements are intended to have in practice. Part 3 explores the literature on strategic management and planning in the public service. Part 4 presents a content analysis of published strategy statements, based on criteria established in the framework for the study. Part 5 reviews the process used in departments and offices to derive and implement strategy statements. Part 6 explores the impact of strategy statements to date and the linkages between statements and key functions such as budgeting and business planning. Finally, in Part 7, conclusions are drawn and recommendations made towards enhancing the impact of strategy statements in public service management.

PART 2

The Formal Position and Framework for the Study

2.1 The pre-legislative situation

Strategy statements were first formally mentioned in February 1994 in a speech by the then Taoiseach, Albert Reynolds, TD. In his speech to government ministers and departmental secretaries he introduced the government's intention to develop strategic management in the Irish public service. He identified three key areas to be addressed: the contribution public bodies can make to national development; the provision of an excellent service to the public; and the effective use of resources. Strategy statements were identified as a central element of the strategic management process. All departments were asked to produce strategy statements clearly setting out their objectives, how these will be met, and how available resources will be used:

> What these statements will do, is to outline where departments should be strategically ... as opposed to where they currently are, and critically, how they will achieve the change required (p. 4).

A key point here is the emphasis on where departments *should* be as opposed to where they are. A primary purpose of strategy statements is challenging the status quo. It is intended that strategy statements are used to point the way ahead after a critical scrutiny of current practice.

The Taoiseach put particular emphasis on the need for senior management in each organisation to *collectively* review and analyse the internal and external factors affecting their organisations:

> This has to be a continuing process, with ongoing monitoring and fine-tuning of action programmes, and a constant clear focus on priority issues and objectives. The (Strategy) Statement must be grounded in this process ...

These Statements of Strategy will be straightforward, well focused, succinct statements – indicating what each organisation will contribute to bettering the overall national goal. They will address how best resources can be concentrated on priority needs. What these statements will not be is a once-off exercise to be forgotten once they're produced. And they will not be a shopping list for extra resources (p. 8).

As a follow-up to this initiative by the Taoiseach, the Department of Finance prepared a framework within which strategy statements were to be devised and progressed. This framework is set out in diagrammatic form in Figure 2.1. The main elements in the framework are:

1. *Strategic review and analysis.* This involves reviewing mandates; analysing the internal and external environments through an analysis of organisational strengths, weaknesses, opportunities and threats (SWOT analysis); and an identification of client interests.

2. *Mission.* Following on from the analysis, each organisation should identify its mission and set high-level objectives for achieving that mission.

3. *Strategic options and choices.* From the mission and the range of options identified to address strategic issues, choices need to be made. Particular strategies are to be identified and selected at this stage, with the strategy statement outlining these strategies.

4. *Implementation.* This involves preparing and initiating action programmes to give effect to the chosen strategies. Divisional objectives and performance targets are to be set, underpinned by appropriate structures, systems and resources.

5. *Monitoring/feedback.* Monitoring of progress against targets and the taking of corrective action is identified as needed in an iterative process. Feedback to identify gaps and inform needed adjustments is seen as part of the ongoing review process and as needed for the major reviews of statements every three years or as required by government.

Figure 2.1: Framework for the Strategic Management Process

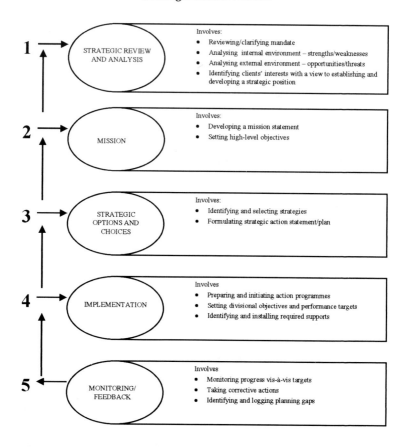

Source: Department of Finance, *Framework for the Development of a Strategic Management Process in the Civil Service*, March 1994, Appendix A.

In 1996, strategy statements were referred to in *Delivering Better Government* (p. 28). Here, in the proposed new framework for authority and accountability which the report outlines, secretaries general/heads of office were identified as being responsible: 'for the preparation on a periodic basis (i.e. every three years) of a statement of the business of the Department, setting out the key objectives and service delivery standards, targets and related strategies and performance measures, together with evaluation procedures'. It was envisaged in *Delivering Better Government* that strategy statements would remain an essential feature of the strategic management process, and would be published and subject to examination by an appropriate Oireachtas committee.

2.2   The Public Service Management Act, 1997, and subsequent guidelines

To give effect to the accountability framework outlined in *Delivering Better Government*, the Public Service Management Act, 1997, sets out the responsibilities of the secretary general of a department or head of office, including:

4(1)(b) at the following times, or at an earlier time if the Minister of the Government having charge of the Department or Scheduled Office so requires, preparing and submitting to the Minister of the Government a strategy statement in respect of the Department or Scheduled Office –

(I)   within 6 months after coming into operation of this Act,

(II) within 6 months after the appointment of a new Minister of the Government having charge of the Department or Scheduled Office, and

(III) at the expiration of the 3 year period since the last such statement was prepared and submitted, and providing progress reports to the Minister of the Government on the implementation of the strategy statement annually or at such intervals as the Government may by order from time to time direct.

Strategy statements are defined in the Public Service Management Act, 1997:

5(1)   A statement referred to in this Act as a 'strategy statement' shall –

(a) comprise the key objectives, outputs and related strategies (including the use of resources) of the Department of State or Scheduled Office concerned

(b) be prepared in a form and manner in accordance with any directions issued from time to time by the Government, and

(c) be submitted to and approved by the relevant Minister of the Government with or without amendment.

(2)   The Minister of the Government shall, not later than 60 days after the strategy statement has been approved, cause a copy thereof to be laid before each House of the Oireachtas.

Speaking at the publication of the Public Service Management Bill, the then Minister for Finance, Ruairi Quinn, TD, outlined his view on the place of strategy statements within the whole new public management framework:

> These strategy statements are important because they will provide a sound basis for civil servants to exercise greater initiative and endeavour in the administration of central government. Management and staff in all departments and offices will be given a clear and consistent understanding of precisely what is expected of them in their jobs. Ministers and members of the Oireachtas will have formal statements of strategy from every department and office which together will form a mosaic of objectives and outputs comprising the business of the public services. Most importantly, the general public, the taxpayers of this country, as clients and customers of the institutions of Government, will have valid and accessible standards for judging levels of quality and performance in the delivery of the public services. These statements will open up the organisation, role, functioning and operation of Departments to public scrutiny to a degree never seen before.

As a follow-up to the publication of the Public Service Management Act, 1997, and the requirement for strategy statements to be produced within six months of the Act coming into operation, in November 1997 the government asked the Implementation Group of Secretaries General to issue guidelines on the preparation of strategy statements by departments and offices. These guidelines have been published (*Link*, 1998a). Building on the framework for the strategic management process developed in 1994, the Implementation Group identify fourteen key elements which they state should be incorporated in strategy statements:

1. Mission statement.

2. Mandate and environmental analysis.

3. Customer/client interests and needs. In particular, the strategy statement should have regard to departmental Customer Service Action Plans developed under the Quality Customer Service Initiative.

4. Identification and management of cross-departmental issues. Each statement should identify and address such issues and the steps to be taken to consult with other departments/agencies.

5. Goals/high-level objectives. These should not exceed five or six in number, and should be outcome-oriented and achievable.

6. Critical success factors. These are the key factors which will determine the success of the department in achieving its outputs.

7. Resource allocation/reallocation issues.

8. Internal capability to realise the departmental goals. Responses to address difficulties identified in areas such as structure, resources and skills and which might constrain goal achievement should be outlined in the strategy statement. Particular stress is placed on the identification of change management resources needed, especially training and development.

9. Embedding the strategic management process in departments. There are two main elements to this:

   a) Business planning process. The need for divisional business plans and their place in implementing the organisation strategy should be recognised and identified in the strategy statement.

b) Civil service change programme. Statements should set out the steps to be taken to develop and implement the action programmes arising from the SMI, such as service delivery, human resource management (HRM), financial management, IT and Freedom of Information. Also, a commitment to consultation and participation in the formulation of the action programme is seen as essential, having regard to Partnership 2000 participation arrangements.

10. Cross-functional linkages within departments.

11. Performance measures/indicators. Strategy statements should set out performance measures and indicators, both quantitative and qualitative, as a basis for assessing departmental performance.

12. Relations with agencies operating under the aegis of the department.

13. Extending the SMI to the wider public service. Departments should set out in their statements steps being taken in respect of organisations operating under their aegis.

14. Monitoring/reporting/corrective action. The framework for monitoring and reviewing progress should be outlined, as should procedures for corrective action.

In February 2000 the fifth social partnership agreement, *Programme for Prosperity and Fairness*, was published by the government. This agreement re-emphasises the key role of strategy statements in the modernisation of the civil service. Particular emphasis is placed on the role of the strategy statement in informing detailed business planning, providing a means of managing performance, and improving the standard of service delivery.

2.3 Framework for the study

From this brief review of formal accounts of the role of strategy statements, it can be seen that the statements are intended to be central to the strategic management process within the civil service. In particular, the formal accounts highlight what is expected of strategy statements in terms of: (a) the *content* of strategy statements; (b) the *process* by which statements are derived and implemented; and (c) the *impact and linkages* which strategy statements are intended to secure in practice. These issues are outlined diagrammatically in Figure 2.2, and provide a framework for this study into the role of strategy statements.

Figure 2.2: Framework for the Study of Strategy Statements

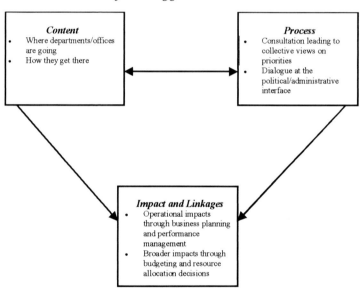

2.3.1 The content of strategy statements

In terms of the content, the main conclusions to be drawn about strategy statements from the formal accounts are that they should focus on where departments and offices should be in the future and on how they are going to get there. Strategy statements have a role in challenging the status quo of programme delivery, emphasising a constant quest for improvement. With regard to where departments and offices should be, the main requirements are that strategy statements will set out:

- An environmental analysis, incorporating an analysis of the strengths and weaknesses of the internal environment and the opportunities and threats posed by the external environment.

- The key objectives, outputs and related strategies (including the use of resources) of the department or office.

- An assessment of customer/client interests and needs and how the department or office intends to respond to these.

- The department's or office's proposed position on identified cross-departmental issues and cross-functional linkages within departments.

With regard to how departments or offices are going to get to where they should be, the main requirements are that strategy statements will set out:

- Performance measures and indicators charting progress against objectives and monitoring and review procedures in general.

- How the strategic management process is to be embedded in the department or office, particularly through the development of business planning, and implementation of the SMI change programme (changing the internal capacity of the department or office to meet the identified strategic objectives).

2.3.2   The process by which strategy statements are produced and implemented

In terms of process, there are four main issues which arise from the formal accounts regarding the development of strategy statements:

- Strategy statements should represent the *collective* views of senior management in each department or office. Rather than have individuals working on their own sections of the statement, it should bring senior managers together to discuss the key strategic issues facing the organisation.

- Strategy statements should be drawn up in consultation with and with the participation of staff of the department or office. Particular regard is to be paid to participation arrangements agreed under *Partnership 2000 for Inclusion, Employment and Competitiveness* (1996).

- Strategy statements are produced by the secretary general of the department or head of office, and passed on to the minister for approval with or without amendment. The minister then places the strategy statement before the Oireachtas. The statement therefore provides a means of dialogue between the secretary general and the minister and the minister and the Oireachtas on the mission and objectives of the organisation.

- Strategy statements are intended to embed the strategic management process into the day-to-day running of government departments and offices. They are meant to give a focus to the SMI change programme.

2.3.3   The intended impact and linkages of strategy statements

With regard to the intended impact of strategy statements and the linkages needed to secure this, the formal accounts indicate three main levels of impact: at the department/office level; at the political/administrative interface; and with the general public.

- At the departmental level, it is intended that strategy statements will provide a clear and consistent understanding to management and staff of what is expected of them over the timespan of the statement. This is to be done through the development of business planning at the division/section level, through the development of performance management at the level of the team and individual, and through the implementation of the elements of the SMI change programme highlighted in the strategy statement.

- At the political/administrative interface, strategy statements are intended to provide ministers and members of the Oireachtas with clear objectives and outputs which give an overview of the business of running public services. This should facilitate the prioritising of issues and resource reallocation decisions. This requires effective linkages between the strategy statement, departmental budgeting process and evaluation practices. The move to multi-annual budgeting, outlined in *Financial Management in a Reformed Public Service* (1999), will obviously be a key influence here in the future.

- At the level of the general public, strategy statements are intended to outline standards against which judgements can be made regarding the quality and performance of service delivery.

PART 3

Literature Review

3.1 Introduction

Strategic management has been defined by Thompson (1997) as:

> ... a process by which organisations define their purpose, objectives and desired levels of attainment; decide on actions for achieving these objectives in an appropriate timescale, and frequently in a changing environment; implement the actions; and assess progress and results (p. 18).

It has also been suggested that strategic planning is not a single concept, but one which embraces a range of approaches (Bryson and Roering, 1989), although there is little agreement in the literature regarding the substance and meaning of the concept of strategic management, since strategy can mean many things to many people (Gunnigle et al, 1997). While most of the literature on strategic planning and strategic management has its origins in the private sector (Bryson and Roering, 1989), recent developments across OECD countries reflect a growing usage of these concepts and their associated techniques in the public sector (Lawton and Rose, 1994). The extent and nature of such developments in countries such as the UK and New Zealand have been described as a shift away from traditional public administration towards a New Public Management (NPM) which places emphasis on, among other things, the role of strategic management in setting and clarifying policy objectives, as well as the adoption of HRM and culture change techniques as a means of providing more effective, responsive public services (Farnham and Horton, 1996). However, while there are numerous models of strategic management, ranging from the highly rational, structured approach to a reactive, *ad hoc* approach, there is a recognition that not all approaches to strategic planning primarily developed in the private sector are applicable to the public sector (Bryson and Roering, 1989).

The purpose of this chapter, however, is not to describe and compare the merits of different approaches to strategic management. Rather the intention is to explore the contribution of the literature on strategic management to some of the key challenges which arise in the formulation and implementation of strategy statements in the public sector. This exploration will facilitate the analysis of progress made by Irish civil service departments in this regard, in the context of the requirements placed on them under the ongoing programme of reform. The following key issues, which are derived from the framework of this study, will be explored:

- The *content* issues inherent in strategic management – in other words, how do public sector organisations ensure that strategic plans reflect their strategic concerns and mandates and the needs of stakeholders in a way in which progress against objectives can be measured?

- The *process* issues implied in strategic management – for example, what part do strategic statements play in determining the relationships between the respective heads of departments and ministers? To what extent are staff involved in the process, and how do organisations ensure that formulated strategies are embedded in the day-to-day activities of the organisation?

- *Impact and linkages* – how are strategies linked with key business issues, including budgetary considerations, detailed business planning and individual objectives? How does reporting on such progress occur?

3.2 The content of strategic management
Before considering in any detail the content of strategic management, it is important to distinguish between its two key stages: strategy formulation and strategy implementation (Elcock, 1996). Strategy *formulation* is a

combination of strategic analysis and choice, the aim of which is to specify the future direction in which the organisation will move. Strategic analysis is concerned with understanding the nature of the organisation's environment (opportunities and threats), evaluating current resources (strengths and weaknesses) and critically analysing existing strategies. Following on from this, strategic choice is concerned with establishing what courses of strategic action are available in the context of the strategic analysis (Thompson, 1997). The second broad stage, strategy *implementation*, is concerned with ensuring that the organisation has the right structures, processes and culture to carry out its formulated strategies. It is important to recognise, however, that these aspects of strategic management do not take place in distinct sequential stages, nor are they simply a description of a future desired state (Elcock, 1996; Poister and Streib, 1999; Bryson and Roering, 1989). Rather, strategic management can be seen as a complex, iterative management process involving a series of learning cycles and intermediate states which provide an overall guiding framework to assist individuals and groups in their day-to-day decision making. The relevance of this from a public sector perspective is highlighted in Poister and Streib's definition of public sector strategic management which they argue entails:

> ... managing a public agency from a strategic perspective on an *ongoing* basis to ensure that strategic plans are kept current and that they are effectively driving other management processes (p. 310).

Thus, strategy formulation does not end when implementation begins. Rather, mechanisms must be put in place to ensure that strategies can be continuously adapted to changes in the internal or external environment. The interdependency of the two stages will be borne in mind throughout the remainder of this discussion.

3.2.1 Environmental analysis

The content of an organisation's strategy is usually derived from an analysis of its strategic position, and the identification of appropriate strategic choices. Most organisations commence strategy formulation with strategic analysis. If the strategic plan is to reflect the mandate of the organisation and the needs of its stakeholders, a systematic assessment of internal strengths and weakness, and external opportunities and threats, (SWOT analysis), should be carried out. This process can also be assisted through the undertaking of a PEST analysis which is an assessment of the political, economic, social and technological trends in the organisation's environment. Regardless of the techniques used, it should be borne in mind that the purpose of strategic analysis is not simply to describe an absolute list of internal/external factors. For example, environmental opportunities, such as buoyancy in the national economy and demographic change, will simply remain *potential* opportunities unless the organisation actually identifies and utilises resources to take advantage of them. The real purpose of strategic analysis is to identify ways in which internal strengths (for example, technology, strong management team) can be used to specifically exploit external opportunities or to minimise external threats, and to minimise or remove identified internal weaknesses (for example, rigid working practices, skills deficiencies) (Thompson, 1997). Organisations must also factor in sufficient flexibility within strategies to ensure that they can be adapted to changes in the external environment. For example, in a public sector context, demographic changes will affect demand for a range of social services such as housing, schooling and healthcare.

3.2.2 Strategic choices and objectives

Having assessed key external and internal issues, strategic choices should be identified. The choices made are usually given effect through the setting of high-level goals and objectives, which are translated into divisional objectives. There is a common recognition in the literature that the setting of objectives in the public sector is less straightforward than in the private sector, given the multiple and often conflicting demands of a range of different stakeholders (Elcock, 1996; Stone and George,

1997). For example, strategic choices may be shaped and in many cases pre-determined by government commitments to particular policy approaches or choices. This is not necessarily a criticism of the public sector *per se*, but rather a realistic reflection of the context within which strategic choices and corresponding objectives must be determined.

Notwithstanding these constraints, there is a consensus in the literature that objectives should be realistic, challenging, timely, measurable and actionable. They must not be so broad as to be meaningless in terms of being translated into measurable action. A number of writers have suggested that in the public sector, there is a tendency for strategy statements to be too broad-ranging and ambitious in relation to desired strategic objectives, with the resulting danger that 'if everything is strategic, nothing is strategic' (Clarke and Stewart, 1991: p. 74). In other words, if nothing is prioritised, managers try to do too many things at once, which dilutes the intended impact of strategy. Hay and Williamson (1991) stress that the formulation and implementation of strategy must by definition involve trade-offs, since objectives must be prioritised in terms of what is financially and operationally feasible. The implications of this argument are that organisations must systematically assess both the desirability and feasibility of objectives *before* making strategic choices. This issue will be explored further below.

3.2.3 Use of performance indicators

In setting out objectives, it is also important that organisations identify measures which can be used to chart and measure performance in relation to the achievement of objectives. In the private sector, external pressures compel organisations to provide cost-effective quality service, since consumers can, in most cases, record dissatisfaction with services by choosing an alternative service provider. In contrast, it is often argued that in the public sector it is more difficult to measure performance in view of the multiple, conflicting and often intangible nature of objectives and the monopoly position of service providers. Thompson (1997) illustrates this with a useful example.

The performance and effectiveness of an education system relates to the impact on pupils after they leave school, on their parents, on taxpayers who fund education, and on future employers. However the perspectives of these different groups will differ, which makes it very difficult to quantify and measure effective performance of the department concerned. It is far easier to measure related issues such as examination performance, building occupancy, pupil/teacher ratios, but such measurement would not take into account the broader impact on key groups in society. Thompson (1997) suggests that notwithstanding these limitations, public sector organisations can develop mechanisms to measure many aspects of performance. For example, they can begin by distinguishing between performance indicators, which should be used to assess aspects of service that are difficult to measure, and performance measures or targets, which should be used to measure quantifiable outcomes. In the case of objectives that are difficult to measure, a public sector organisation might also consult with its clients to ascertain how effective they perceive the quality of its services to be, particularly since clients may have no means of exiting the relationship which they have with the service provider.

3.2.4 Addressing the needs of stakeholders
Most strategic management models stress the need to take into account stakeholder interests during the strategy formulation process. A stakeholder can be seen as 'any individual, group or other organisation that can place a claim on the organisation's attention, resources or output, or is affected by that output' (Bryson and Roering, 1989: p. 16).

In the context of the public sector this definition embraces a wide range of groups, including customers, taxpayers, unions, employees' interest groups, political parties and other governments. The need to satisfy such a diverse range of stakeholders can considerably complicate the strategy-making process by comparison with the private sector. Given the wide-ranging, and often conflicting, interests of stakeholders and the need for accountability in the public sector environment, it has been suggested that it may be necessary to adopt a much more systematic and formal approach to consulting with stakeholders than may be appropriate in the private sector (HM Treasury, 1991). For example, in the case of clients or customers, mechanisms such as customer surveys, customer panels, community consultation and complaints patterns can be employed to assess what customers expect and how they perceive the quality of services delivered (Clarke and Stewart, 1991; Humphreys et al, 1999). Recognition of stakeholders' interests and needs are usually given formal effect in the strategic plan. There is also a need, however, to ensure that the strategic planning process is flexible enough to respond to changing needs and perspectives of stakeholders.

3.2.5 Interdepartmental co-operation

While the need for organisations to develop greater inter-organisational relationships is not a central concern of mainstream strategic management literature, there is an increasing awareness that strategic management in the public sector can be enhanced through greater collaboration with other public sector organisations. This is of particular importance in view of the increasing evidence of policy issues which 'cut across departments and levels of government' (Boyle, 1999; see also Clarke and Stewart, 1991). Indeed some authors have suggested that the co-operation of other public sector organisations may be a critical factor in the realisation of strategy (Elcock, 1996). Thus, patterns of interdependence must be identified and appropriate means of communication and decision making must be devised among the players involved. As with stakeholder interests, it is important that resulting cross-departmental strategies are embedded in the strategic management process.

There is also a need for effective internal co-operation and collaboration, for example among different sections or divisions of an organisation. For example, cross-functional teams may be set up as a means of tackling complex problems, which span different functions or tasks, through the sharing of complementary skills and expertise. The success of team-based activities, however, is very much dependent on a range of factors, including commitment to a common approach, and skilled and committed leadership (see Boyle, 1997b, for a more detailed discussion of team-based working in the public sector).

3.2.6 Statement of strategy

The end product of the strategy formulation process is usually a formal statement of strategy or a corporate plan. Thompson (1997) suggests that formal statements of strategy can provide a useful mechanism for assisting managers in understanding where they fit within the strategic planning process. However, as with the strategic management process itself, the strategy statement should not be seen as definitive or inflexible, but rather as a mechanism that can be used to provide guidance to organisational members and a synthesis of the important strategic issues. In other words, the production of a strategic plan is not simply an isolated annual event. Rather, it should be viewed as something which is subject to a constant process of re-examination and, where necessary, adjustment in response to changing environmental or business needs (Simpson, 1998).

3.3 The process of determining strategy

A key issue in the literature focuses on the question: who is responsible for formulating strategy? The literature suggests that while the success of implementation depends on all employees, the leader of an organisation plays a vital role in the process, since s/he is usually in a unique position to gather and receive information about all aspects of the business and has responsibility for ensuring that appropriate structures and policies are in place for carrying out strategy (Thompson, 1997). While private sector concerns usually relate to determining the roles and responsibilities of the chairman and chief executive respectively, a similar dilemma exists in the public sector, in which dual leadership can be seen to be exercised by political and administrative leaders. In this regard, it has
.

been suggested that strategic management is made more difficult in the public sector because of the shorter-term considerations of politicians, in contrast to the longer-term perspective of the head of a department (Lawton and Rose, 1994). Even if this view is valid, however, it is not necessarily an argument for abandoning the process of strategic management in the public sector. Rather it suggests that an organisation should have the required capacity to respond to changes in strategy in the event of political change.

Organisations also need to consider the extent to which its members are to be involved in the strategy-making process. Simpson (1998: p. 478) argues that 'strategy is best done collectively by a fairly large group of people at multiple levels of the organisation'. There is an increasing recognition in the literature that for a change initiative, of which strategic management is a prime example, to succeed there is a need to involve employees in the process, in contrast to the traditional top-down approach to managing change (Beer et al, 1993; Rashford and Coughlan, 1994). The rationale is that unless staff are consulted in the formulation of strategy they will have inadequate ownership of change, which may undermine the implementation of strategy. To address this issue, involvement of employees might be facilitated through the creation of workshops or working groups set up to examine and analyse the implications of a particular area of strategy.

3.4 Implementation, impact and linkage issues
If strategy formulation is difficult, the process of realising and implementing strategy is an even more challenging one. As discussed in Part 2, the intended impact of strategy in a public sector context can be seen to occur at three levels: the organisation, the political/administrative interface, and the general public. The focus in this discussion will be on the first of these levels, since this will affect the impact at the other two levels. While the benefits of involving organisational members in the formulation of strategy have already been discussed, their role assumes an even greater importance in the implementation stage, since strategy will

only secure its intended impact if it provides an understanding to management and staff of what is expected of them, and if it informs and guides the day-to-day activities of employees. This requires the translation of high-level and divisional objectives into individual objectives, and the monitoring of achievements against progress. It also requires an assessment of the organisation's ability to match internal capacity to strategy (Hardy, 1994; Clarke and Stewart, 1991). A number of key internal factors will now be considered insofar as they illustrate the key challenges involved in ensuring that strategy informs the activities of the organisation and secures its intended impact.

3.4.1 The 'people issues'

The first organisational issue which must be strategically aligned to ensure that strategy implementation takes place concerns the 'people issues', since it is argued that 'people are the key to implementing strategic management or any other change process' (Vinzant and Vinzant, 1996: p. 144). The need for HRM strategies to be aligned with business strategy has been a common theme of the HRM literature since the 1980s (Fombrun et al, 1984; O'Brien, 1998). Yet the reality is that few organisations accord a strategic role to the management of human resources and there can often be a misfit between HRM policies and business strategy. For example, McKevitt (1998) suggests that very often in public sector reform programmes an incorrect assumption is made that managers will have the required capability to respond to desired changes. He adds that little attention is given to skilling or re-educating managers to enable them to adjust behaviours and working patterns which in many cases have been built up over many years.

Attention also needs to be given to the integration or fit among the different policies. This is usefully illustrated by means of an example. If an organisation wishes to develop greater use of interdisciplinary teamwork to assist in the achievement of a particular objective, existing HRM policies which emphasise the use of individually based reward systems and seniority based promotions systems may dilute the intended impact of the objective concerned, since such policies will conflict with a team-based approach to work. Similarly, in the absence of a systematic performance management system, it is difficult to translate business goals to the individual level as a means of ensuring ownership and measuring progress. If an organisation has systematically analysed its internal strengths and weaknesses and has considered these issues in the light of its intended strategies and objectives, it should be possible to identify areas requiring change in relation to HRM policies.

3.4.2 The role of organisational culture

Another element which may require strategic alignment if strategy is to have its intended impact is organisational culture, since an organisation's culture can play a key role in assisting, or alternatively hindering, the implementation of strategy. The interest in organisational culture stems primarily from the excellence writings of the early 1980s (Peters and Waterman, 1982; Deal and Kennedy, 1982). One of the key claims of research carried out by Peters and Waterman (1982) is that strong, cohesive, organisational cultures lead to excellent performance. Conversely, however, it has been argued that strong cultures can actually act as a barrier to change, because of the entrenched positions and behaviours of their members (Smither et al, 1996). The potential for organisational culture to act as a barrier to the implementation of strategic management may be particularly strong in the public sector, since, as Vinzant and Vinzant (1996: p. 145) point out, 'the implementation of strategic management in the public sector often requires profound changes in culture, requiring people to adopt markedly different values and styles of thinking'.

In the context of this discussion, what is of importance is the extent to which the behaviours and values of organisational members are aligned with or supportive of the intended strategy. Since strategy very often requires a change in the way things are done, it follows that organisational culture may also have to change. In an analysis of the strategic management process in the UK local government sector, Clarke and Stewart (1991) suggest that the commonest yet most fundamental mistake made by most organisations in the strategic management process is to ignore the need for organisation development, a term which can be broadly used to refer to any process of planned change in an organisation. While it would be outside the scope of this study to consider in detail what Clarke and Stewart refer to as the centrality of organisation development to the strategic management process, it is worth observing that since strategic management implies change, there is a need to develop and manage a planned programme of change to ensure that the organisation has the required internal capability and willingness to meet the challenges of strategic management. In the absence of a planned approach to change, resistance, which may be passive or active, may arise (Rashford and Coughlan, 1994), which will undermine the implementation process.

3.4.3 Ensuring the right structure

A final element which may require greater alignment with strategy is organisational structure. McKevitt (1998) suggests that there is a need to focus critically on whether public sector organisations are structured to most effectively deliver services. Alignment with strategy is particularly challenging in an organisation which has a traditional hierarchical structure, since employees may be insufficiently empowered to identify with corporate goals. In recognition of this issue McKevitt (1998) suggests that professional bureaucratic structures, typically found in public sector organisations, may require restructuring to enable managers to operate and make decisions with the necessary flexibility and autonomy. As a consequence, there is increasing evidence of the use of more flexible and responsive organisational forms to encourage greater ownership of strategic issues, including cross-disciplinary teamwork, quality circles, greater delegation of power, and innovative uses of IT to flatten decision making and improve communications (Hardy, 1994).

3.4.4 Financial/budgetary capability

An assessment of an organisation's internal capacity to achieve strategy necessitates an examination of the financial resources available. In other words, an organisation's desired strategy must be rooted in what is financially feasible. In the public sector, this consideration may be made more difficult by the fact that while it may be possible to cost activities, the absence of a profit motive relaxes the constraints placed on the organisation to produce outcomes in an efficient and effective manner. Thompson (1997) suggests that in the absence of a profit motive the emphasis in the public sector should be on outcomes and need satisfaction, with money acting as a constraint on what is possible rather than acting as an objective itself. The danger is that where the focus is on outcomes rather than inputs, an organisation's strategy statement may be overly ambitious in setting out its desired objectives. It has been suggested that this may be particularly problematic in times of economic growth, in which there is a tendency by public sector organisations to focus on the benefits and outcomes of policies and objectives, with insufficient attention being paid to the costs involved in producing desired outcomes or to the resources available (Lawton and Rose, 1994).

The foregoing concerns emphasise the importance of linking the strategic management process to the financial management process in the public sector. To assist this process, Lawton and Rose (1994) suggest that there are three critical success factors:

- The timing of the strategic planning process must coincide with the budget preparation process.

- The strategic plan itself must correspond with the organisation of the budget.

- Budget staff must be able to collect, analyse and present information that supports the strategic management process.

They also suggest that organisations who are experienced in budget planning processes will have less difficulty implementing strategic management than those who do not. Such an observation is encouraging in the context of the Irish civil service, given the well-established traditions of the annual estimates and budgetary processes that effectively dictate the limits of capital and current expenditure in civil service departments. However, familiarity with financial planning on its own is not sufficient. What is required is that organisations are capable of making the link between strategies and objectives and the financial planning process (Bryant, 1997).

3.5 Conclusions
A range of inter-related challenges inherent in the process of strategic management have been considered in this discussion.

The key challenges and issues can be usefully summarised as follows:

- Environmental analysis must meaningfully inform and influence the setting of objectives and strategies, and sufficient flexibility must exist to adjust strategies to take account of further external changes.

- Formulation of desired strategies implies trade-offs, and a prioritisation of strategic choices.

- Notwithstanding the difficulties frequently implied in a public sector context, it is important that organisations establish performance indicators or measures to assess the achievement of objectives and strategies.

- Cross-departmental issues need to be incorporated into the setting of objectives and strategies.

- Involvement by staff in the strategy formulation process can play a role in reducing resistance to change, and as a consequence, ensure greater ownership of strategic change.

- The implementation of strategy is enhanced through the strategic alignment of HR policies with business strategies.

- Strategic management implies a change in organisational culture and as a consequence there is a need for organisations to plan and manage the process of cultural change.

- To assist in the implementation of strategy, organisational structures need to be critically assessed and where necessary realigned or remodelled, for example through a team-based approach.

The central theme which has emerged is that strategic management is not a simple once-off event. Rather it is a complex, iterative, change process which requires careful management and planning. As a consequence there is a need for organisations to plan carefully for the changes implied in strategic management, and to ensure that adequate flexibility exists to adjust strategies in response to changing mandates of key stakeholders. The literature also suggests that the development of strategic HR policies and strategies can play a critical role in ensuring that an organisation has the capabilities required to meet the challenges implied in the process of strategic management.

PART 4

Analysis of the Content
of Strategy Statements

4.1 Introduction

In this chapter, the focus is on a content analysis of the strategy statements produced and published to date. Two sets of statements are assessed: those published in 1996 prior to the introduction of the Public Service Management Act, 1997, (the 1996 statements) and those published in 1998 (the 1998 statements). It is important to bear in mind that the 1996 statements were preceded by unpublished 1994 statements, which influenced the approach to and content of the 1996 statements. Annex 1 lists the strategy statements reviewed for this exercise.

Before going into the issues involved, it is important to note that an assessment of the content of strategy statements does not necessarily give a full picture of the state of strategic management in government departments and offices. As will be addressed in Part 5, the *process* of strategic management is in many ways equally as important as the content, if not more so. Formal, written statements do not necessarily capture all that is going on. Also, this assessment is not meant in any sense as a ranking of strategy statements. Statements may serve varying functions in different government departments and offices. However, given these caveats, it is of no doubt that content is important. Strategy statements represent the main means by which the Oireachtas and citizens generally can assess and engage with a department's strategic direction. Unless the content of statements is clear and comprehensive, it is doubtful that they will inform either external assessment or internal management practices.

The criteria against which strategy statements are assessed are those outlined in section 2.3.1, derived from the guidelines issued to departments and offices. The issues covered are: conduct of environmental analysis; identification of key objectives, outputs and related strategies; assessment of customer/client interests; position on cross-departmental and cross-functional linkages; use of performance measures; and embedding the strategic management process.

4.2 Conduct of environmental analysis

A fundamental building block of strategic management is the conduct of environmental analysis. The framework and guidelines for strategy statements developed centrally indicate that statements should include an analysis of the internal and external environments, through the conduct of a SWOT (strengths, weaknesses, opportunities and threats) analysis. The identification of client/stakeholder interests and issues is a key task, with a view to developing an appropriate strategic position. This latter point is particularly important: environmental analysis is not conducted for its own sake, but rather to identify and define the critical issues to be faced. The environmental analysis should inform and contextualise the remainder of the strategy statement.

In reviewing the strategy statements, a first point to make is that, in general, there has been an improvement in the level of environmental analysis carried out between the 1996 and 1998 statements. This point is also raised by Keogan and McKevitt (1999). Several departments have notably improved their analysis. For example:

- The 1998 statement of the Department of Education and Science contains a more substantive analysis of the implications of, and challenges arising from, the environmental analysis.

- The Department of the Taoiseach in 1998 includes a comprehensive section covering both the external and internal environments, describing changes taking place.

However, there are still some weaknesses with the environmental analysis in many of the statements. Two main weaknesses are identified:

- In some statements, the environmental analysis tends to take the form of a simple listing of issues. There is no subsequent analysis of the implications of these issues for the operation of the department/office.

• Allied with this point, but even in some cases where some analysis is carried out, there is often an absence of a clear linkage between the environmental analysis and the objectives and strategies outlined in the statement. The analysis does not seem to inform the rest of the statement. Rather, the sense is purveyed of a SWOT analysis undertaken as an end in itself, because it is a requirement.

The more successful of the strategy statements do not display these weaknesses, and develop clear linkages between their environmental analysis and the objectives and strategies contained in the statement. A prime example here is the Department of Public Enterprise. Both their 1996 statement (as the Department of Transport, Energy and Communications) and their 1998 statement have a very comprehensive external environmental analysis. First, the general strategic context and issues common to all commercial state companies under their aegis are covered. Then, each individual sector, for example transport or energy, has its own sectoral analysis identifying the main issues. The sectoral objectives and strategies then flow from this analysis in a consistent and coherent manner. Similarly, the Department of the Environment and Local Government's 1998 statement contains a detailed analysis of internal and external factors, and displays a good linkage between the issues discussed and the implications for strategy. The Department of Agriculture and Food have a comprehensive environmental analysis in their 1996 statement (as the Department of Agriculture, Food and Forestry) which clearly informs the rest of the statement, as detailed by McKevitt and Keogan (1999).

One interesting feature of the Department of Justice's 1996 statement, not repeated in 1998 or replicated in any other statement, is a short two-page summary of where the Department expects to be 'Five Years Ahead'. Drawing on the environmental analysis, this section outlines where the Department sees itself as being in 2001 (for example, more policy driven; publishing policy statements and commissioning research; having delegated many operational responsibilities to other agencies in the justice area). This exercise usefully contextualises the issues drawn from the environmental analysis.

Summary of review of environmental analysis

Standard generally good overall, with improvement from 1996 to 1998. Environmental analysis is undertaken to some degree in all statements. The main weaknesses concern:

- *a tendency in some statements to list issues, without sufficient follow-on analysis of the implications*

- *a failure in some cases to clearly develop the linkages between the environmental analysis and the resulting objectives and strategies.*

4.3 Identification of key objectives, outputs and related strategies

The Public Service Management Act, 1997, specifies that a strategy statement shall '... comprise the key objectives, outputs and related strategies (including the use of resources) of the Department of State or Scheduled Office concerned ...'. The guidelines issued by the Implementation Group further indicate that a small number of goals/high-level objectives should be incorporated in strategy statements, and that they should be outcome-oriented and achievable.

All departments and offices have at their core some outlining of goals, objectives and strategies. Some improvement between the 1996 and 1998 statements is noticeable overall, with the 1998 statements in general showing a higher degree of clarity and specificity. Taking

Ordnance Survey Ireland as an example, in their 1996 statement, objectives and strategies tend to be set out as fairly general statements. In 1998, specific targets are added which are often quantified.

One notable feature is the wide range of terminology used to describe activities and the varying number of different levels of specificity used. To take some examples:

- Goals, strategies (Agriculture and Food)

- Key result areas, measurements, action plan (Civil Service Commission)

- Objectives, key outputs, strategies (Revenue Commissioners)

- Objectives, strategies, outputs (Justice, Equality and Law Reform)

- Objectives, critical success factors, measures, strategies, targets (Valuation Office).

The extent to which this diversity of use of terminology is an issue depends on the degree to which cross-comparison between statements is needed. If statements are primarily stand-alone, the use of common terminology is not of such great significance. However, if looking for issues or trends across statements, the varying terminology can be confusing.

A further issue related to terminology is that there is no consistency as to how departments or offices define and use terms like goals, objectives and strategies. There is most commonality around the term goals, which usually are fairly high-level statements covering broad issues. However, objectives and strategies tend to be defined and used in different ways. Some objectives tend to be more like goals; general statements of intent (for example, to promote and co-ordinate government policies in the x sector). Others are relatively specific and results-oriented (for example, to promote and safeguard the employment rights and occupational safety and health of workers; to achieve 95 per cent uptake in primary childhood immunisation programme). Many items under the heading of strategies read as if they are objectives, and in practice in some statements it is difficult to draw a practical distinction between what is outlined under objectives and strategies.

Whilst it is probably unwise to be too precise and prescriptive about differentiating among goals, objectives, strategies and the like, recognising that some degree of overlap is inevitable, nevertheless some differentiation is needed if the different terms are to be meaningful. Drawing from good practice examples in the strategy statements, a hierarchy from the general to the more specific can be discerned:

- *Goals.* Generally fairly broad statements of intent, outcome focused, covering a particular sector or sphere of activity.

- *Objectives.* More specific statements of intent which indicate how the goals are to be achieved. May be outcome or output focused, or both. Defined in such a way that they are capable of allowing subsequent assessment as to whether or not they are achieved. May sometimes usefully be supplemented by specific targets.

- *Strategies.* Detailed actions to be pursued in order to achieve or to support the achievement of goals and objectives.

- *Outputs.* The goods or services produced as a result of pursuing the specified goals and objectives. May be either generic outputs for an office or section, or specific outputs arising out of objectives and strategies.

Illustrative examples of goals, objectives, strategies and outputs, taken from a variety of strategy statements, are outlined in Table 4.1. Annex 2 contains an extract from the *US Department of Education Strategic Plan, 1998–2002* as a further illustration of goals, objectives and strategies: the US government has pioneered outcome-oriented goal setting under the Government Performance and Results Act, 1993.

Some goals and objectives are of such a nature that their achievement is outside the direct control of any

Table 4.1: Illustrative Examples of Goals, Objectives,
Strategies and Outputs

Goals

To promote the growth of a competitive, consumer-orientated and added-value food processing sector (Department of Agriculture and Food).

To promote fairness and efficiency in the labour market thereby maximising employment, protecting the welfare of workers and promoting social inclusion (Department of Enterprise, Trade and Employment).

Objectives and Associated Strategies

Contribute to enhanced appreciation by the public of issues affecting poor countries (Department of Foreign Affairs)

- work with the National Committee for Development Education to increase understanding of the causes of poverty in the developing world and what Ireland and the international community can do to help.

Improve the level of oral health in the population overall (Department of Health and Children)

- set oral health targets for key age groups and establish an oral health database for monitoring changes in oral health.

Outputs

The number of projects facilitated through the coastal zone management process (Department of the Marine and Natural Resources).

Establishment of a 'carding system' to support high performance athletes (Department of Tourism, Sport and Recreation).

---

department or office (for example, secure international competitiveness). In such circumstances, it is important that intermediate outcome goals and objectives, against which department/office performance can be assessed, are detailed. Also, there is a need for recognition that achievement of outcomes may be influenced by factors outside the direct control of the department/office. In this context, the 1996 statement of the then Department of Tourism and Trade contains a useful section on factors outside the Department's remit which might impact on target achievement over the lifetime of the statement (see also the discussion in section 4.6 below on the use of performance measures).

One interesting variation among strategy statements is that some set out objectives and strategies for each division of the department or office, while others group objectives and strategies not by division but by some other means. The Office of the Revenue Commissioners, for example, set out eight programmes in their 1998 statement, five business programmes and three business support programmes. In either case, what is important is that high-level objectives and strategies are set which are likely to last over the period of the statement.

A central intention of the Public Service Management Act, 1997, and the guidelines, is that the resources needed to achieve goals, objectives and strategies be covered in strategy statements. The resource implications of actions pursued, and resource allocation and prioritisation decisions, can then be assessed in a coherent way. It has to be said that the coverage of resources is a significant weakness in the strategy statements as they stand at present. Many statements make no reference to resources at all. Of those that do, several refer to their annual budget expenditure and staffing levels, but do not link these references to their goals, objectives and strategies. It is thus impossible to determine to what extent actions in the statements represent a wish-list, or reasoned and costed actions which have been prioritised in some sense.

Some statements do attempt to explore the implications of resources for the strategic direction proposed, but often in a tentative manner. For example, the Department of Agriculture and Food's 1998 statement has a section on resources that indicates what resources there are and how they are being allocated in line with the strategy statement. The Department of Justice, Equality and Law Reform's 1998 statement, in its objectives for the Garda Síochána, management of offenders and the courts, indicates its 1998 expenditure allocation and staffing levels involved in each case.

By way of contrast to the general lack of information in statements, in the US, as illustrated in Annex 3 taken from the Department of Education's strategic plan, the resources allocated to the achievement of each strategic goal are detailed as far as is practicable.

On the general issue of highlighting key objectives, the Department of Justice, Equality and Law Reform's 1998 statement uniquely has a useful section entitled 'Summary of Government Commitments'. Here, the main objectives in the Government's *Action Programme for the Millennium* and *Partnership 2000 for Inclusion, Employment and Competitiveness,* which the Department has responsibility for or is involved in, are outlined. The link to the relevant reference in the strategy statement is indicated. This allows quick access to see what actions are proposed under key government commitments.

Summary of review of identification of key objectives, outputs and related strategies

All statements address this issue. The main goals, objectives and strategies for departments are generally clearly set out and reasonably well specified. The main weaknesses concern:

—   *confusion of terminology, and lack of consistency in differentiating and developing linkages among goals, objectives, strategies and outputs*

—   *some goals and objectives are not clearly outcome and results focused, or capable of being assessed for impact*

—   *little or no discussion of the resources needed or resource implications regarding the achievement of goals and objectives.*

4.4 Assessment of customer/client interests and needs

Customer service is one of the cornerstones of the SMI. Providing an excellent service to the public was one of the three key areas highlighted at the establishment of the SMI in 1994. Reflecting this prioritisation, it would be expected that customer service would feature prominently in strategy statements. The guidelines indicate that statements should include an identification of customer/client interests and needs, and outline initiatives to improve service delivery. In particular, attention should be paid to the Customer Service Action Plan developed under the Quality Customer Service Initiative.

Given this level of commitment to service to the public, it has to be said that the overall impression gained from the coverage in strategy statements of customer service is relatively disappointing. On the positive side, the Quality Customer Service Initiative has led to an improvement in many statements from 1996 to 1998. Most statements now have a specific piece on customer service, either as one of the main goals, or as a separate section in the statement. Customer service is often identified as a priority area for action.

However, there are two main limitations apparent in the coverage of customer service in many strategy statements. First, while many statements refer to their Customer Service Action Plan, there is often little sense of this action plan informing the strategy statement. Rather, the impression is given that the two are separate exercises. This raises some concerns about the centrality of customer service in practice. Second, there is often little evidence of assessment of customer/client needs driving the development of objectives and strategies. Some statements refer to the fact that they are/will be carrying out need assessments, but there are few signs that many statements have yet been informed by such analysis. These issues emphasise the point made by Humphreys (1998: p. 77) that '... in many bodies still, despite the national initiatives already taken and the rising expectations amongst external customers themselves, a genuine commitment to addressing the needs of the general public remains relatively low in the pecking order of managerial priorities compared, for example, to meeting the internal political demands of the system'.

Given these general limitations, some statements do make particular contributions towards improving service delivery. The Central Statistics Office, for example, covers the issues of customer expectations and customer focus in its 1998 environmental analysis. This analysis is followed through by the development of a business support programme focusing on customer service and statistical quality, which in turn contains specific objectives and performance indicators. The Department of the Environment and Local Government's 1998 statement includes a fairly detailed discussion on customer interests and needs, with reference made to specific targets outlined in the Customer Service Action Plan. There is also recognition of the need to build on existing initiatives in developing improved mechanisms for structured dialogue with key stakeholders in each of the Department's areas of responsibility.

Both the 1996 and 1998 statements of the Department of Social, Community and Family Affairs are strongly customer-oriented. They identify values or guiding principles for dealings with customers, and the 1998 statement proposes the development of a new service delivery model, together with the setting out of detailed service standards for clearance times, customer service, and control.

A further interesting feature of the 1998 Department of Social, Community and Family Affairs statement is that it recognises the importance of internal customers as well as external customers. The statement proposes the piloting of service level agreements between different areas of the Department. Similarly, the Department of the Taoiseach give prominence to internal as well as external customers. The need to set internal service standards to support the delivery of objectives is recognised.

The difficulties of defining a customer in the public sector context (Humphreys, 1998) are sometimes highlighted. Both the Department of Agriculture and Food's and the Department of Tourism, Sport and Recreation's 1998 statements contain a paragraph recognising that the demands made by different clients may on occasion conflict with one another, and that ultimate accountability is to the citizen and taxpayer, through the minister and the Oireachtas, rather than to particular interest groups.

Summary of review of assessment of customer/client interests and needs

The Quality Customer Service Initiative has led to an improvement in the coverage of customer interests in the statements. Overall, however, coverage of this issue is disappointing given its centrality to the SMI. Two main weaknesses concern:

- *the absence of linkages between Customer Action Plans and the development of objectives and strategies in the strategy statements*

- *little evidence of the assessment of customer/client needs underpinning and informing the strategy statements.*

The more informative statements draw on customer/client expectations and needs (including internal customers) and develop appropriate actions deriving from these needs.

4.5   Identification of cross-departmental issues and cross-functional linkages

The ability of the civil service to deliver quality services is often dependent on good co-operation among different departments and among sections/divisions within departments/offices. The guidelines for strategy statement preparation indicate that cross-departmental issues should be identified, along with the role the department/office plays, and how it will interact with other departments/offices to achieve government policy. With regard to cross-functional linkages, the guidelines indicate that cross-over points should be identified, together with the 'whole of organisation' approach being adopted.

There is significant improvement in coverage of this issue in the 1998 statements compared to the 1996 statements. This probably reflects the growing importance of cross-cutting issues as a topic (Boyle, 1999). In the 1996 statements, cross-departmental and cross-functional issues tend to be mentioned barely at all. In the 1998 statements most departments/offices have sections which explicitly refer to cross-departmental and cross-functional linkages. For example, the 1996 statement of the Department of Education and Science (the then Department of Education), whilst recognising the importance of liaison with other departments by listing the other departments it works with, does not develop this issue or link through to strategy in any way. There is no reference to cross-functional linkages. The 1998 statement has a much more comprehensive coverage of cross-departmental issues, and an informative section on cross-functional linkages.

It is common for departments/offices to highlight specific cross-departmental issues and to identify and list other departments/offices involved in the management of such issues. However, few statements take the further step of outlining how they will develop co-operative efforts, other than in the most basic terms, for example through listing inter-departmental committees they are involved in. Similarly, with regard to cross-functional linkages, while many (though far from all) statements identify specific cross-over issues, this is often done in a general way, with the need to improve co-operation highlighted, but less detail on how improved co-operation is to be achieved.

With regard to cross-departmental issues, the more informative statements identify specific issues, detail the other agencies involved, and give a sense of how the issues are to be addressed. They also outline the implications for objectives and strategies generally. For example, the Department of the Environment and Local Government's 1998 statement covers the interrelationship with other departments and agencies as part of its environmental analysis. This general analysis is then followed through by the outlining of key interrelationships for each sector, in the context of the detailing of goals and strategies. The Department of Justice, Equality and Law Reform's 1998 statement highlights three specific cross-agency issues – crime, children and equality – and indicates the main concerns, who is involved, and what role the Department will play. For example, with regard to crime, specific areas to be addressed are identified, including developing a stronger research base on predisposing factors in crime and the need for joint examination of such research findings and follow-through by the relevant departments and agencies. This issue is further highlighted as a specific objective in the statement, with associated strategies and outputs.

The Department of Social, Community and Family Affairs' 1998 statement contains a useful appendix which details specific cross-departmental issues, other departments/agencies involved, and actions required by the Department. An extract from this appendix is shown in Table 4.2. Such a table usefully highlights cross-departmental issues and the types of actions needed to encourage a cross-departmental approach.

With regard to cross-functional linkages within departments/offices, several statements refer to the need to develop cross-divisional teams and an increasing emphasis on teamwork generally. The more informative statements indicate how and where such cross-functional linkages will be applied. The Department of Public Enterprise's 1998 statement, for example, indicates how cross-divisional

Table 4.2:
Extract of Cross-Departmental Issues from the Department of Social, Community and Family Affairs

Issue	Department/ Agencies Involved	Action Required by DSCFA
Combating Unemployment		
• Encourage the maximum take-up of the unemployed of work opportunities (whether in the open economy or on special schemes)	DSCFA, D/ET&E, FÁS	Practical co-operation on the ground with FÁS to maximise referral opportunities
• Encouraging the unemployed to take up education/training	DSCFA, D/Ed&S, FÁS	Co-operation in relation to availability and accessibility of educational/ training opportunities
• Developing an Employment Support Service for customers	DSCFA, D/Ed&S, FÁS, D/ET&E	Co-operation in relation to providing more employment opportunities.
• Influence development of taxation system to minimise work disincentives	DSCFA, D/Fin, Revenue, D/ET&E	As opportunities arise (e.g. Tax Strategy Group) stress importance of focusing tax relief on the lower paid in line with the recommendations of the Expert Working Group on the Interaction of the Tax and Social Welfare Systems
• Removing disincentives to work caused by interaction of a number of schemes	DSCFA, D/H&C, D/E&LG, D/Ed&S, D/Fin	Prepare proposals regarding reducing disincentive effects of secondary benefits following completion of study on this topic
Voluntary and Community Sector		
• Promote a coherent framework of statutory support of the voluntary and community sector	DSCFA, D/ET&E, FÁS, D/E&LG, LAs, D/H&C, D/TS&R, D/JE&LR	Publication of White Paper

Source: Department of Social, Community and Family Affairs, 1998.

co-operation has been strengthened by the introduction of a system of sectoral reviews, for example interrelationships between gas and electricity policies have become clearer. The statement also highlights other issues where cross-divisional teamworking is becoming increasingly important, such as corporate governance, the monitoring of annual reports, and implementation of the Freedom of Information Act. The 1998 statement of the Office of the Revenue Commissioners indicates that for certain cross-cutting strategies where divisions need to work together, specified co-ordinating responsibility will be given to a designated strategy manager.

Both the Department of Education and Science and the Department of Arts, Heritage, Gaeltacht and the Islands highlight a range of internal arrangements which are being developed to enhance cross-functional co-ordination. Such initiatives include the establishment of a principal officers network (both departments), co-ordination by internal working groups (Education and Science) and the establishment of an SMI co-ordination group, chaired at assistant secretary level, to co-ordinate the change programme within the department (Arts, Heritage, Gaeltacht and the Islands).

**Summary of review of identification of cross-departmental issues
and cross-functional linkages**

A significant improvement in coverage of these topics from 1996 to 1998. Cross-departmental and cross-functional issues are, by and large, identified and other departments or divisions involved listed.

The main weakness concerns the failure in many statements to move on from simply identifying issues and listing those involved. The best statements also highlight what needs to be done, and how, in order to secure and improve co-operation and co-ordination.

4.6 Specification of performance measures

The guidelines state that strategy statements should include performance measures and indicators, both quantitative and qualitative. There is recognition that this task is not a simple one, and that not everything will be achieved in the first iteration.

It is clear that a number of departments and offices have found the development of performance measures a challenging task. Overall, performance measurement is probably the weakest aspect of strategy statements to date. As with the other topics covered, some improvement is evident between the 1996 and 1998 statements. For example, the Central Statistics Office and the Department of the Marine and Natural Resources make little or no mention of performance measures in their 1996 statements, yet make notable improvements in this area in their 1998 statements. This suggests that improvement is possible and that, as implied by the guidelines, it may take a number of iterations before the issue is addressed comprehensively. However, even while improvements have been made, it is evident that there is still some way to go.

Almost one-third of strategy statements include few or no performance measures or indicators in their 1998 statements. Of those that do, two particular weaknesses which are evident are the limited specificity of many measures/indicators and the limited range of activities covered by measures/indicators.

With regard to the specificity of measures/indicators, many items included under the category of performance indicators in statements are rather vague and ambiguous. Indicators such as 'actions taken', 'review on a timely basis', 'enhancement of skills of staff', 'effective representation of Ireland's interests', are not sufficiently detailed to provide a useful picture of progress toward achieving specified objectives and strategies. This issue is linked to the clarity of goals, objectives and strategies. The clearer and more specific these are, the easier it is to develop clear performance measures, and vice versa.

With regard to the range of activities covered, while many plans have at least some measures and indicators, few consistently include a comprehensive set that focus on the results aimed for through objectives and strategies. Many indicators focus on timeliness issues – complete report by x; publication of green paper by y – rather than on the desired outcomes and intermediate outcomes. Also, in general, as Keogan and McKevitt (1999) point out, there is a lack of focus on the interests of customers and clients, with more focus on management interests.

Despite these difficulties, some departments and offices have taken significant steps in developing performance measurement in their strategy statements. The Valuation

Office, the Office of the Revenue Commissioners and the Department of Social, Community and Family Affairs in particular have comprehensive and detailed performance measures included in their 1998 statements. The Valuation Office uses the balanced scorecard (Boyle, 1996; 1997a) as a performance management tool which, as the 1998 statement indicates: '... allows an organisation to supplement traditional output/financial measures with criteria which monitor performance from the perspective of the customer, internal business processes and learning and growth'. The Revenue Commissioners have developed a system of key performance indicators which are clearly associated with each of the strategies. While some of these indicators are fairly general in nature, many are specific and quantified. The process for reviewing and reporting on indicators is also set out, and it provides a good understanding of how performance reporting will occur. The Department of Social, Community and Family Affairs' 1998 statement sets out service standards covering clearance time, customer service and control, outlining targets which are both actionable and assessable. They also indicate steps being taken to develop performance indicators in relation to a number of specific topics: outcomes, quality, accuracy, internal customer service, and staff.

These three cases are organisations largely tasked with executive functions (though notably not all their measures are related to executive functions; they also address issues such as policy, quality and HRM). Statements from departments with a mix of policy and executive functions and which attempt to develop comprehensive performance measurement systems include the Departments of Agriculture and Food and the Marine and Natural Resources. Here, indicators are specified for each sectoral policy and operational goal, and linked to objectives and strategies (more explicitly for Agriculture and Food in their 1996 statement – then the Department of Agriculture, Food and Forestry – than in their 1998 statement). Examples of smaller offices which set out detailed and comprehensive measures in their 1998 statements are the Central Statistics Office and the Office of the Ombudsman.

One interesting feature in some statements is the inclusion of longer-term outcome goals and measures. For example, the Department of Enterprise, Trade and Employment has a competitiveness goal at the heart of one of its three main performance measures: to improve Ireland's position in the World Economic Forum Competitiveness League, in which it ranked eleventh in 1998. The Department of Finance's 1998 statement includes economic growth in excess of the EU average as one of its indicators of success in the area of expenditure policy.

Such outcome measures, while particularly welcome in strategy statements aiming at longer-term end results, raise a couple of questions as to their role. First, as such measures are outside the direct control of individual departments, it is likely that intermediate outcome measures will be needed to enable assessment to be made of departmental contribution to their achievement. Second, department officials clearly cannot be held responsible for the achievement of such outcome performance indicator results. But such indicator results are important in assessing progress. What is likely to be needed here is to hold officials directly accountable for intermediate indicator results directly within their control. They should also be accountable for the collection and use of outcome indicator results outside their direct control. If, for example, economic growth does not proceed in excess of the EU average, managers would be expected both to know this and to ascertain what new strategies are needed as a result.

Summary of review of specification of performance measures

Performance measurement is the weakest aspect of strategy statements to date. Particular weaknesses concern:

- *the lack of clarity and specificity with regard to many of the measures included in statements, and the absence of clear links to goals, objectives and strategies*

- *the limited range of activities covered by performance measures.*

The best statements are those where goals, objectives and strategies are focused on results. They clearly link measures to objectives and strategies, and develop measures for a wide range of activities, including outcomes and quality.

4.7 Embedding the strategic management process

The literature review highlights the fact that the implementation of strategy is dependent on an organisation's capacity to align itself with the strategies, through structural, policy and cultural adjustments. The aim is to ensure that managers and staff at all levels adopt a strategic management approach to business, not seeing the SMI as an add-on to existing work. The guidelines highlight two main elements in terms of embedding the strategic management process: the development of divisional business plans to translate strategies through to team and individual objectives; and the implementation of the civil service change programme, covering such issues as service delivery, HRM, financial management, IT, freedom of information, and partnership. The guidelines also emphasise the need for statements to indicate how departments/offices plan to adjust their internal capacity to achieve their goals, with a particular emphasis on proactive HRM.

Again, as with all the other issues covered, there is a notable improvement in coverage of this issue between 1996 and 1998. For example, in its 1996 statement, the then Department of Enterprise and Employment sets out objectives for support areas, for example IT, HRM. The 1998 statement takes this further by discussing the Department's internal capacity to achieve its goals, and setting out a number of success factors seen as critical to the implementation of the statement. Strategic goals and objectives are set out, to assist the Department in implementing change.

The main weakness in statements in addressing this issue is similar to one highlighted with regard to environmental analysis: a tendency in some statements to list issues and actions to be taken without integrating these issues with the rest of the statement. So, while all statements address the issue of embedding the process to one degree or another, in some cases this reads as an add-on to the statement, put in largely because it is required. The actual linkage between strategies and the consequent need to readjust internal capacity is not apparent from the statement.

The more informative of the statements clearly show how thinking on embedding the process is influenced by the strategic review undertaken and strategies chosen to be pursued. In the 1998 statement of the Department of the Taoiseach, for example, internal critical success factors are identified for the achievement of the major goals, and five key elements of internal capability needed to realise the internal critical success factors identified: people, effective internal service standards, the implementation of performance management, the determination of performance indicators, and financial management and resource allocation. An action programme is outlined in the statement to address these issues. Similarly, the Department of the Environment and Local Government's 1998 statement contains a section on implementation which details the internal change programme required to address weaknesses identified in the internal analysis. Particular emphasis is put on the business planning process as a means of going beyond and beneath the sectoral goals.

With reference to business planning, and its role in embedding strategy statements in particular, the statement of the Office of the Revenue Commissioners contains a useful outline of what they intend to be covered in business plans. Two main sections for each business plan are envisaged: recurrent activities, outlining the normal business activities of each division; and development activities, containing specific action plans aimed at delivering on strategies outlined in the strategy statement. The Department of the Taoiseach includes divisional business plans as an appendix to its 1998 strategy statement.

Relating to broader organisational change issues, the 1998 statement of the Department of Justice, Equality and Law Reform contains a useful section on organisation change and development. This maps out the changes proposed, and a timetable for their achievement. The benefit of setting out in broad terms the organisational changes needed is that the relationship between organisational and business changes is made clearer.

Summary of review of embedding the strategic management process

All statements address this issue to some degree. Proposals for business planning, partnership arrangements and internal capacity building are generally outlined. The main limitation concerns the extent to which the embedding process as outlined is drawn from and linked to the environmental analysis and emergent strategies – in some statements there is little evidence of this.

The more useful statements clearly link the embedding process with the rest of the statement, and outline both structural and process changes aimed at ensuring the achievement of established goals.

4.8 Conclusions

This review of the content of strategy statements shows significant improvements in the quality of statements overall from 1996 to 1998. The 1998 statements tend to cover a more diverse range of issues, and in greater depth, than the 1996 statements. However, significant limitations with the statements still exist, and there is scope for improvement in further iterations.

PART 5

Analysis of the Process Issues

5.1 Introduction

In Part 4, it was pointed out that since the content of strategy statements does not necessarily give a full picture of the state of strategic management in departments and offices, it is necessary to focus also on the process of formulating, and subsequently implementing, strategy. This chapter focuses on the key issues and challenges implied in the process of strategic management. As with the preceding chapter, the analysis focuses on two sets of statements: those published in 1996 prior to the introduction of the Public Service Management Act, 1997, (the 1996 statements) and those published in 1998 (the 1998 statements). A certain amount of information regarding the process undertaken by departments and offices is evident from an analysis across the broad spectrum of departmental statements. However, these statements do not capture the organisational dynamics involved in formulating and implementing strategy. As a consequence, it is necessary to supplement this analysis with a more detailed consideration of the issues, challenges and experiences encountered at organisation level. Interviews were carried out in the four departments selected for more in-depth research in this study, and the findings from these interviews are considered throughout this chapter.

At the outset of this analysis, it is important to re-iterate the distinction between the two key but interlinked strands involved in the process of strategic management which were explored in detail in Part 3. The first strand refers to the strategy *formulation* process by which the statement of strategy is produced. The second refers to the strategy *implementation* process, during which strategy is realised or embedded in the day-to-day activities of the organisation. The research findings will be considered under these two broad headings.

5.2 Strategy formulation

In the context of this study, two key issues are identified in Part 3 in regard to the strategy formulation process: the respective roles of ministers and secretaries general (heads of departments), and the role of employees in the strategy formulation process. In relation to the first issue, most of the 1996 and 1998 statements commence with introductory statements by both the minister and secretary general concerned. These introductory statements do not however provide an indication of the respective roles of the parties concerned. However, the more in-depth research undertaken in the selected departments suggests that the dual leadership role is not perceived to adversely affect the strategic management process. There is a sense in most departments that heads of departments are 'left to get on with the business of implementation' by their respective ministers. The view was also expressed that the Public Service Management Act, 1997, which provides a legal clarification of the roles and responsibilities of both the minister and secretary general, has enhanced the strategic management process, by clarifying and strengthening the authority, responsibility and accountability of the secretary general in regard to the implementation of strategy.

At the same time, there is a recognition that where new priorities are identified at a political level, there is an implicit understanding that these will be addressed, giving rise in some instances to a reordering of priorities and resources. Such instances do not appear to present major problems for the departments concerned. In some cases, political input was seen as a real strength, for example in securing resources to meet strategic priorities. Finally, a concern was raised in Part 3 regarding the potential conflict between the relative permanence of the administrative leadership in the public sector, in contrast to the sometimes short-term perspective of politicians' and the implications of this conflict for the strategic management process. However, the Public Service Management Act, 1997, puts in place a formal process of continuity, by stipulating that new statements should be prepared within a six-month timescale, in the event of a change of minister in a particular department.

The second issue relates to the role of staff in the strategy formulation process. The literature reviewed in Part 3 suggests that involvement of staff at this stage is crucial, as it ensures greater ownership of the changes implied by strategic management and as a consequence such ownership has the potential to enhance the success of strategy implementation. The use of consultative mechanisms is held to be particularly useful within a bureaucratic organisational structure, since it is argued that such mechanisms 'lie outside the usual hierarchical lines of decision making and communication, and allow a more problem solving and open-minded exploration of issues and possibilities for action' (Joyce, 1999: p. 96).

The mechanisms employed by departments and offices range from those of a highly participative nature, in which staff are actively involved in formulating strategies, to more traditional top-down approaches, in which staff appear to have little input into the process. For example, it is worth noting that in the 1998 statements, roughly one-third of departments and offices make no reference to the role, if any, played by staff in the strategy formulation process. Of the remainder, in a significant proportion of cases, references to the role of staff in the strategy formulation process are either vague or minimal. While it is not possible to assume that minimal or no reference to such a role meant that departments did *not* consult with staff, it is important to recognise the benefits of not only involving staff, but also formally *acknowledging* the role played by staff in the process.

Those departments that specifically describe and acknowledge the role played by staff in the strategy formulation process outline a range of mechanisms employed to this end. Several departments set up cross-functional working groups, for example to consider strategies under a particular heading or theme. Others engaged initially in a top-down approach where, typically, senior management prepared an initial draft statement. In many cases, staff were then engaged or consulted in the process, for example through workshop-based discussions. A number of departments engaged external facilitators to assist in the strategy formulation process. In some cases, facilitators were employed throughout the strategy formulation process; while in others, they were engaged at particular stages of the process, for example in the delivery and facilitation of staff workshops.

It is also worth noting that the number of departments that acknowledge the role of staff in the 1998 statements represented a significant increase on the number that did so in the 1996 statements. From this one might conclude that in the case of a number of departments, greater efforts were made to involve and/or formally acknowledge the role played by staff in the strategy formulation process. For example, in the Central Statistics Office, the Department of Education and Science, and the Department of Enterprise, Trade and Employment, no references are made in the earlier statements to the role, if any, played by staff in the strategy formulation process. In contrast, in the recent statements, all three acknowledge the role played by staff, for example, through participation in workshops or staff meetings.

The interview findings reveal a variety of related approaches to involving staff in the strategy formulation process, and some features of these approaches are worth considering in more detail. For example, in the Office of the Revenue Commissioners, during the production of its earlier statement and the more recent process of formulating the 2000–02 statement, staff participated in working groups in order to devise strategies for particular high-level issues. In both instances, membership of the groups comprised staff from across grades and divisions and locations. However, in the more recent exercise, an open invitation was extended to all staff to participate in a working group of their choice, in contrast to the earlier exercise in which staff were selected to participate. This approach was taken as a means of encouraging greater staff participation. In addition, in the more recent exercise, chairpersons (who were at assistant secretary level) were not assigned responsibility for working groups which were dealing with their own area of expertise. This was felt to be useful in that they could bring a greater degree of objectivity and 'freshness' to their chairing role. A number of chairpersons also commented as to how impressed they were by the high calibre and abilities of staff who were involved in the process, which highlighted the enormous potential among staff within the organisation.

Cross-representative consultation was also a feature of the approach taken in the Department of the Marine and Natural Resources. During the strategy formulation process undertaken to produce the 1997–99 statement by the then Department of the Marine for example, task forces were drawn up from across functions and grades to prepare reports on a range of strategic issues. Membership of these groups comprised a mix of volunteers and people who were 'co-opted' on to particular groups. Divisional heads also played a significant role in the process. The Department also engaged an external facilitator for a number of months to assist the work of the various task forces, and this was seen to be a valuable addition to the process.

In contrast, the approaches taken in the Department of Enterprise, Trade and Employment and the Department of the Environment and Local Government were more divisionally based. In the Department of Enterprise, Trade and Employment, each division set up a group to develop divisional strategies, in addition to which an overall cross-divisional group was set up. In the Department of the Environment and Local Government, a document outlining the proposed structure of the statement was prepared by the management advisory committee (MAC) and a cross-divisional liaison group and circulated to all staff. Cross-divisional workshops were then held for senior officers, who in turn organised sectional discussions with their own staff (where group discussions would have presented serious logistical difficulties, discussions were held with representative groups). The output of these discussions was fed back to the MAC and liaison group.

There was a recognition in a number of departments that even with a participative process in place, it is not possible to reflect the views of all staff. To address this issue, in the case of both the Office of the Revenue Commissioners and the Department of the Environment and Local Government, an invitation was extended to all staff to make submissions on particular strategic issues if they wished to do so.

A common concern in a number of the departments, including the Office of the Revenue Commissioners and the Department of Enterprise, Trade and Employment, centres on balancing the tension between keeping the thrust and content of the statement at an appropriately high level and the need to recognise and describe the day-to-day contribution of all areas of the department. The concern was expressed that divisiveness and resentment might arise where all contributions are not recognised. At the same time, there is a view that the strategy statement is not necessarily the most appropriate vehicle or forum for recognising the comprehensive contribution of various divisions and sections. In the Department of the Marine and Natural Resources for example, in addition to fulfilling its requirements under the Public Service Management Act, 1997, the production of an annual report is seen as a formal and appropriate means of recognising the contribution of each division and all staff in the organisation. In addition, many departments and offices are using their business plans to reflect in more detail the work of divisions and sections.

A related concern centres on the need to meaningfully engage staff in the strategy formulation process. Concerns were expressed that consultative processes might be perceived by staff as mere 'public relations exercises'. The interviews reveal a recognition of a certain degree of cynicism among staff as to how meaningfully they are actually involved in the real process of strategic management. In the Department of Enterprise, Trade and Employment, subsequent to the production of the statement, a feedback exercise was undertaken to ascertain the views and perceptions of clerical and executive staff regarding their role in the strategy formulation process, the results of which suggested that there was a need to involve staff more fully in future exercises of this kind. The feedback obtained also highlighted the need for clear linkage between the statement of strategy and business plans as a means of informing the day-to-day work of staff.

Notwithstanding this concern, in some cases, despite initial cynicism, staff found their involvement in the formulation process to be enjoyable and challenging. Ultimately however, from a strategic point of view, there is a view in some departments that not every recommendation made by a working group can be taken on board, yet inevitably there may well have been such an expectation within a group. The experiences encountered by one department suggests that where all proposals are not taken on board, there is a need to provide effective feedback to staff, for example to outline why certain strategic actions were or were not agreed upon.

5.3 Strategy implementation

A recent OECD review of public sector reform programmes suggests that successful reform is as much about having a well-conceived implementation strategy as it is about the design of reform (OECD, 1999). Part 3 examined a number of organisational issues which influence the implementation of strategy. In particular, HRM, cultural and structural issues are identified as key areas which require alignment and adaptation if they are to fit with business strategy. Each of these will now be considered.

5.3.1 People issues

The extent to which strategy is successfully implemented is significantly dependent on the organisation's employees, since 'people are the key to implementing strategic management or any other change process' (Vinzant and Vinzant, 1996: p. 144). Frequently however, there may be a misalignment between HRM policies and business strategy. For example, once a business strategy has been agreed, the organisation may need to assess the desired competencies or behaviours required of staff against the existing profile of the organisation. Measures might then be put in place to develop the required competencies and skills to enable staff to fulfil strategies or actions.

At central level, the HRM agenda for reform is seen as one of the central planks of the wider reform process in the

Irish civil service, and the impact of this agenda at
departmental level is recognised in many of the 1998
statements. For example, many departments acknowledge
that the implementation of a centrally agreed performance
management system, and the development of proposals at
central level to greater professionalise the individual HR
function and devolve responsibility for HR matters to line
managers', represent both opportunities and potential
challenges at departmental level.

A recognition of the need for a greater integration of
departmental HRM policies with business strategy is
evident from most, but not all, of the statements reviewed.
Some departments, such as the Department of Public
Enterprise and the Department of Defence, have already
undertaken consultative processes to develop HR strategies
to complement the strategic management process. In other
departments, commitments are made to ensuring a greater
alignment between HR strategy and corporate strategy. For
example, the Department of Social, Community and Family
Affairs recognise that the achievement of strategic goals will
depend critically on their ability to improve the capabilities
of the organisation, and that HRM policies should be
developed as an integral part of corporate planning. This
integration is evident from their more detailed business
plans, in which they identify the HR issues and polices
arising from each set of divisional strategies. Similarly the
Department of the Marine and Natural Resources has set
up a HR strategy steering group to oversee the formulation
and implementation of a HR strategy, with the aim of
achieving the Department's strategic goals through
enhanced HR policies.

In a general sense however, there are a number of
inconsistencies and weaknesses in the consideration of
people issues in the statements. For example, as part of the
strategic management process, many departments carried
out a SWOT analysis, during which they identified internal
weaknesses, which in many cases related to the capability
of staff to deliver on departmental objectives. However, very
few linked the implications of this analysis to the
development of high-level HR strategies, for example to

address internal weaknesses or strengthen internal capability. In addition, in many of the statements, references which are made to HR goals and policies are not particularly helpful in clarifying what measures will be undertaken to ensure a greater fit with strategy. For example, many statements contain commitments to 'provide training for staff' or 'equip staff with the required competencies' with no detail provided as to what competencies or training needs are implied by particular strategies or objectives. Similarly, in some statements, while performance measures are outlined for training and development strategies, they are of limited use. For example, measures include 'number of training days provided' and 'staff attendance at courses' or 'to increase spending on training and development to the centrally recommended target of 3%'. Measuring the return on investment in training in quantifiable terms, while signalling commitment to staff development, does little in terms of ensuring a fit between human resource development and the attainment of business strategy, nor does it say anything about the quality of training to be provided or the added value it will provide in securing the implementation of strategy.

Numerous references were made throughout many of the interviews to the need to better align people issues with business strategy, and in most cases, it was acknowledged that this is both the most significant and the most challenging aspect of the strategic management process. While many believe that the centralised nature of many aspects of HRM, for example in relation to recruitment and selection and to reward systems, limits the extent to which departments can align their HR and business strategies, there is also a recognition that they have the ability to better align training and development and internal promotions systems with their business strategy.

5.3.2 Culture/change
The literature reviewed in Part 3 suggests that any form of organisational change is both a complex and challenging process. Strategic management should by definition imply

the need for organisational change, particularly since 'the implementation of strategic management in the public sector often requires profound changes in culture, requiring people to adopt markedly different values and styles of thinking' (Vinzant and Vinzant, 1996: p. 145). As a consequence, there is a need to plan for and carefully manage the change process. This is recognised at central level, as evidenced by the provision of a central change management fund which is available to departments to assist them in implementing particular change initiatives in the context of the SMI.

An analysis of the statements highlights varying degrees of recognition of the need for planned organisational change during the strategy implementation process. Most of the statements refer to the changes in organisational culture which are required in order to implement strategy, but very little detail is provided as to how this change might be managed. Many departments have set up central strategic or corporate management units to co-ordinate the strategic management process across the department. In other cases, such as the Department of Finance, a change management working group was in operation to advise management on the development of the SMI process. This group has since been replaced by the departmental partnership committee. The interviews reveal strong awareness in many cases of the need for a planned structured approach to change, and an awareness of the challenges involved in managing change. In recognition of this issue Revenue, for example, in their 1997–99 statement include a strategy to establish a central change management consultancy service to assist in the implementation of change.

Resistance to change is an inevitable part of any change process (Coughlan, 1991), and in many organisations, the existence of sub-cultures, for example within areas or grades, may result in differing reactions to change. A review of public sector reforms in OECD countries suggests that there is a need in any change programme to identify and manage sources of resistance (OECD, 1999). The interviews reveal a recognition of this issue. For example it was suggested in some departments that while there may be support for the changes implied by strategic management at senior levels, it can be difficult to translate ownership of change and to achieve the desired changes in behaviour and competencies throughout the organisation. A concern was expressed by a number of interviewees that many middle managers may perceive the strategic management process as an unnecessary burden on the real business of the organisation, and there is a danger that such attitudes can render the process a 'meaningless paper exercise'. It was suggested that the introduction of a performance management system has the potential to embed the process more and enhance ownership and accountability in relation to corporate and divisional objectives.

The literature also suggests that participation can reduce resistance (Coughlan, 1991), and most departments refer to the potential for the new partnership committee structure to assist in enhancing participation and as a consequence, ownership of change. Partnership 2000 (1996: p. 71) suggests that partnership should be an 'open, co-operative process based on effective consultation and participation', in contrast to an adversarial approach to change. The potential for partnership to assist the strategy implementation process, and the wider agenda for reform, is strengthened by the fact that full and ongoing co-operation with change, through the implementation of specific action programmes, will be a pre-condition of certain clauses of the Partnership 2000 public sector pay agreement. It is too early, however, to assess the extent to which this potential will be realised. There is also a tension raised in some of the interviews, between a desire to encourage wider participation and ownership regarding the strategy statement, and the need from a senior management perspective for the statement to challenge existing ways of working.

Finally, recent OECD research also suggests that there are a number of other critical success factors for managing and implementing culture change successfully. In particular it is suggested that motivated and experienced leadership at the highest level in the public sector is vital for implementing all types of reform. The findings of this research state that while visible political commitment is central to any process of change in the public sector, ultimately strong and effective leadership *within* the public sector is vital if change is to be successfully implemented. (See OECD, 1999.)

5.3.3   Structural issues

The literature reviewed in Part 3 suggests that structural changes may be required to embed the strategy-making process in an organisation, and to greater empower employees to take ownership of strategic issues. Organisational restructuring as a means of reducing bureaucracy and improving flexibility is a common feature of reform programmes in many OECD countries (OECD, 1999). A range of mechanisms is available to achieve this aim, including departmental restructuring, the use of cross-disciplinary teamwork, quality circles, greater delegation of power in the organisational hierarchy and innovative uses of IT to flatten decision making and improve communications (see Hardy, 1994 and OECD, 1999). It is suggested that strategic planning can in fact create additional communication channels to those in the hierarchical line, thus creating a more positive culture in terms of flexibility and innovation (Joyce, 1999). At the same time, the interviews reveal a concern that the benefits achieved in involving staff in the strategy formulation process, for example through the use of task forces, are not always realised at the strategy implementation stage. The rigidity of reporting, grading and work structures and systems may result in a lack of identification with corporate and divisional goals and objectives.

A concern was also expressed by some interviewees that, in some cases, high-level strategies or objectives 'overlap' divisions, yet the rigidities of reporting arrangements and work systems can undermine the shared achievement of strategies. These concerns are highlighted by Joyce (1999), who suggests that within a bureaucratic structure, each stratum of the organisation becomes isolated from those above it and below it, and such isolation enables it to develop its own goals, and ignore the corporate ones. The potential for isolation along divisional lines is recognised, for example in the Department of the Environment and Local Government, and they propose to consider how the benefits gained from holding cross-disciplinary workshops during the strategy formulation process can be used on a more regular basis as a means of creating greater awareness of each division's concerns.

An earlier Committee for Public Management Research (CPMR) study highlights the challenges involved in creating permanent work teams in traditional hierarchical work organisations, and attention must be paid to putting in place clear objectives, structures and accountability requirements if teams are to operate effectively 'alongside the traditional hierarchy' (Boyle, 1997b: p. 23). The nature of activities carried out by a department may also affect the extent to which structure impacts on the achievement of strategy. For example, in the Department of the Marine and Natural Resources the secretary general and management team have taken the view that the wide-ranging and overlapping nature of divisional activities means that a team-based approach to the achievement of certain strategies is needed if the strategies are to be pursued effectively.

Efforts to better align organisational structures and systems with corporate goals are evident in a number of other departments. For example, the Department of Social, Community and Family Affairs highlight the need for the development of a new service delivery model, centred around the customer, if they are to achieve their high-level strategic objectives. They also plan to use IT to promote cross-organisational service delivery, through the Reach project. As Humphreys et al (1999) note: 'The aim of Reach is to achieve improved customer service delivery through a greater integration of social services delivered by different departments and agencies, aided by information technology'. Similarly, in the 1997–99 statement of the Office of the Revenue Commissioners, a key strategic issue relates to how best they can align their structure and systems with business strategy, and there is an awareness that a 'root and branch' examination of the organisational structure is required. There is also a recognition that such changes require alterations in the HR systems and significant consultations through traditional industrial relations structures and partnership committees to ensure acceptance of change. Revenue have committed themselves to examining their structures, systems and practices to ensure that they meet business needs. Other departments have also recognised the need for greater alignment of organisational structure with business strategy.   For example, in the Central Statistics Office it is recognised that there is a need to address the difficulties caused by demarcations among different areas and grades in the organisation and a need to promote greater flexibility and teamworking.

5.4 Conclusions

The foregoing analysis highlights a number of key concerns in relation to the process of both formulating and implementing strategy statements.   Firstly, while involvement of staff in the formulation process can play a role in enhancing ownership of the strategic management process, there is a need to ensure that such an exercise is seen by staff to be a genuinely consultative process. At the same time, there is a need for the strategy statement to be sufficiently high level and focused in nature, which may make it difficult to recognise all contributions by staff. Where this arises, it is important to communicate with staff to ensure that they continue to perceive their role in the process as meaningful. Secondly, the development of the appropriate internal capacity required to secure strategy implementation may require change to the organisational culture. As a result, there is a need to adopt a planned approach to managing internal change, including changes to existing HR systems and organisational structure. The findings suggest that the alignment of HR systems and organisational structures with business strategy is the most challenging yet critical element of strategy implementation.

PART 6

Impact and Linkages

6.1 Introduction

It should be noted here that the primary focus in this chapter is on the operational impact and linkages of strategy statements. In the timescale of the study, and given the relative newness of strategy statements as a management tool, it is not possible to make any assessment of the ultimate impact of strategies contained in strategy statements. The difficulties involved in untangling the various causal factors involved in determining the outcome of strategies would also make this a challenging task. We are looking here at the impact strategy statements are having on departmental and office management, particularly through the development of linkages with the business planning process. It should also be noted that it is a senior management perspective that informs the issues outlined here.

6.2 Overview of progress

In general terms there is a very positive response from senior managers interviewed in the course of this study regarding the impact of strategy statements on the running of departmental business. One key point stressed by several respondents is the need to see the strategy statement as part of a process rather than as an end in itself. Its value lies in facilitating prioritisation of issues and the development of change management in departments and offices more than in its intrinsic worth as a stand-alone document. The actual fulfilling of the legal requirement to produce a strategy statement could have been done with relatively little effort, but departments in the main have chosen to use the opportunity to look not only at what they are doing, but also at why and how they are doing it.

The fact that managers have a more explicit statement of what it is they are trying to achieve is also cited as a benefit. In particular, the move to a more collective view by senior management of the direction of the department, noted in the previous chapter, is seen as a positive development. Some departments note the beginnings of a more collegial approach to resource allocation, with greater willingness to consider moving staff from one area to another as priorities develop. This is not universal, and is viewed as still a long way from perfect. But the strategic management process is seen as encouraging such trends in some departments.

Similarly, the strategy statement and associated business plans are viewed as helping to facilitate structured dialogue with ministers on resource allocation and priorities. Ministers, while retaining political direction of departments, are now in general more aware of the resource implications of new priorities they wish to promote. The need to give lower priority to some activities in order to develop new ones may be put on the agenda more effectively in the context of strategy statements. There is some suggestion that the degree of ministerial involvement influences the effectiveness of such resource prioritisation discussions. The more detached the minister, the harder it is to secure commitment to resource reallocation decisions. The more involved the minister is, the danger is that he/she becomes involved in minutiae at the expense of strategic direction. There seems to be a happy medium, whereby there is ongoing dialogue between the minister and the management team, but day-to-day management issues are left to the management team.

In general, strategy statements are seen as giving a greater emphasis to the management of departmental and office business. This is being pursued in particular through the business planning process, to which we now turn.

6.3 Linking strategy statements and business planning

Many managers identify the business planning process as the crucial link between strategy statements and implementation. It is through the business plan for divisions and sections that issues such as the transfer of high-level strategies to actions, budgets and resource allocation, and the development of performance indicators, are most directly addressed.

In July 1998 the Implementation Group of Secretaries General issued guidelines to apply across the civil service in relation to the business planning process (*Link*, 1998b). With regard to business plan format, the main elements required of business plans are:

- A degree of consistency fostered by a common template, to facilitate comparison and co-ordination at the level of the whole organisation.

- The specification of business objectives for the division, clearly linked to higher-level goals and strategies outlined in the statement of strategy.

- Identification and listing of divisional outputs to achieve these objectives.

- Identification and outlining of the expenditure implications of required objectives and outputs, and of support services resources required.

- The specification of individual/team responsibilities for achieving the objectives and outputs.

- Performance indicators to facilitate the monitoring of progress against objectives and targets.

- An identification of linkages, both inter- and cross-departmental, and how these are to be handled.

- Identification of Quality Customer Service implications of the identified objectives and outputs as appropriate.

- Identification of human resources, financial management and IT implications of the plan.

From the point of view of this study, a key feature is the linkage of divisional business objectives with the higher-level goals and strategies in the strategy statement. Most departments attempt to ensure an explicit linkage. For example, in the Department of the Environment and Local

Government each business plan has two parts, the first focused on developing actions related to the statement and the second for other activities. In the first part, divisional business plans must set out each relevant strategy from the strategy statement and link their activities to these strategies. Each activity has an associated target or performance indicator and a statement setting out who else is involved (either cross-divisional or cross-departmental linkages). There is a clear linkage back to strategies contained in the strategy statement.

With regard to resource use, the more clearly business plans can identify the programme and administrative expenditure implications of activities or groups of activities, the more effective the link with the budgetary process. This is an area that departments recognise as needing further work. The absence of expenditure or staff resource information in many instances makes it difficult for managers to assess relative priorities, the resource implications of pursuing particular courses of action, and the value for money obtained from activities.

In general, developing linkages among strategy statements, business planning and resource allocation is a crucial but time-consuming task. In order to maximise integration among the various activities, departments and offices need to ensure that these activities are seen as working together rather than as separate activities. Annex 4 illustrates how the Department of Public Enterprise maps out the timescale of the various activities relating to strategic management in the department. Such a framework can be used as a tool to encourage managers to think through the implications of the linkages for management practice.

6.4 Reporting on progress

An essential element in the implementation of strategy statements is reporting on progress. It is through feedback and reporting, both formal and informal, that the impact of statements can be assessed and encouraged.

Most departments appear to have some kind of monthly reporting on progress at divisional level, linked to progressing the business plan objectives and targets. At senior management level, reporting tends to be either monthly or quarterly. In the Office of the Revenue Commissioners, for example, each division sends quarterly reports of progress against business plan objectives to the Corporate Management Division. They in turn produce a deviation report based on this information which goes to the Board of the Revenue Commissioners. This deviation report highlights targets which have not been achieved – it is taken as read that all others have been met. In the Department of the Environment and Local Government each division prepares monthly reports which go to the secretary general. These monthly reports note progress against activities identified in the business plan. The reports also go to the minister, who has periodic formal meetings with senior management from each division, along with the secretary general, to discuss progress. In this way, the political/administrative dialogue on progress regarding implementation of the strategy statement is encouraged.

Several departments operate a system whereby divisional senior management periodically meet with the management advisory committee (MAC) to discuss progress with the business plans (often quarterly). These meetings provide an opportunity for detailed scrutiny of progress, and can be used to highlight key issues such as changes in the environment, the development of cross-divisional and cross-departmental linkages and resource management. Based on discussions for this study, and previous contacts with some departments, a good practice example of questions to be asked at such review sessions is outlined in Table 6.1. These questions cover both content and process issues, and are aimed at encouraging the implementation of actions identified in the business plans as needed to achieve the objectives and strategies outlined in the strategy statement.

6.4.1 Annual reports
Under the terms of the Public Service Management Act, 1997, departments and offices must provide annual progress reports to the minister on the implementation of

*Table 6.1: Questions to be asked of Divisions
regarding their Business Plans*

The changing environment
- What are the most significant external developments impacting on the divisional sector over the last six months? What are the greatest threats and opportunities related to the achievement of deliverables, and how can these be addressed?
- Has the strategy changed in the divisional sector or is it likely to change?

The business plan
- Do the specified objectives and outputs in the plan correspond to the higher-level goals and strategies of the department?
- Have the division's planned outputs for the review period been achieved?
- Are the targets set challenging, specific and measureable? What performance indicators are being used to track progress?
- What are the current priorities of the division? Have these priorities changed?

The management of the division
- How are financial and staff resources deployed by the division? Any changes needed?
- What is the division's strategy for developing staff? How are the support requirements for the area (such as IT, financial management) being met?

Linkages
- How does the division co-ordinate its work with other divisions or other departments/agencies? How are these linkages managed and what issues need to be addressed?
- How well does the plan link with the Quality Customer Service Initiative?

The process of planning
- Was the plan prepared in a consultative/participative manner with divisional staff?
- Are the arrangements set out in the plan for monitoring and review adequate?
- What can be done by the MAC to improve the capacity of the division to continue meeting its deliverables?

---

the strategy statement. Such reports are intended as a means of reviewing progress and enabling an assessment of the impact of strategy statements to be made. The annual report is seen as an important part of the *ex post facto* accountability regime.

The first annual reports produced under the terms of the Public Service Management Act, 1997, were produced in late 1999. From a brief review of these reports, several points emerge:

- A variety of styles of format and presentation is apparent. With some reports, it is difficult to discern the linkage with the strategy statement. With others, the annual report follows the format of the strategy statement, reporting progress against objectives contained in the statements. This latter format gives more clearly a sense of progress with regard to implementation of the strategy statement.

- As would be expected, the reports seek to portray the department or office in a favourable manner. While a positive approach is to be encouraged for morale and other purposes, it would also be useful for the reports to give a sense of problems encountered or targets not met. This would present a balanced picture of performance.

  In this light, the publication of progress against key indicators linked to policy and operational goals by the Department of Agriculture and Food, and the publication by the Office of the Revenue Commissioners and the Department of Social, Community and Family Affairs of their customer service targets and actual performance achieved, is to be welcomed.

- The target audience(s) for the report seem unclear. Some reports appear aimed at the general public, with significant use of graphics, photographs and glossy production. Other reports read more as working documents.

One key point with regard to the role of annual reports is the question of how they are to be used once produced. If they are simply to be published and then have little active interest taken in them, it is likely that their role in promoting implementation of strategy statements will be limited. Significant questions in this regard are the extent to which the annual reports are assessed or audited by some independent agency, and the degree of political interaction with the annual report. In New Zealand, for example, the typical annual report contains a narrative discussion of performance during the year and financial and service performance statements. These statements are audited by the New Zealand Audit Office. In the US, the first accountability reports to be produced under the Government Performance and Results Act, 1993, are due out in 2000. As with the US government departments' strategic plans and annual performance plans, these accountability reports will be assessed by the General Accounting Office (GAO) and the GAO's comments and reports will then be reviewed by Congress, thus ensuring a political input to the process.

6.5 Dealing with unplanned and unexpected events

One significant influence on the impact and continuing relevance of strategy statements is how unplanned or unexpected events are dealt with. Published strategy statements can only give a view of proposed strategies for certain issues at a particular period of time. Issues may change, and new issues may arise over the course of the life of a strategy statement. New political priorities may emerge. Resources may have to be devoted to address a crisis in a policy field. Coping with strategy under such conditions of uncertainty is an important element of the strategic management process. A particular issue to be addressed is how uncertainty is dealt with in the two interlinked strands of the strategic management process: strategy formulation and strategy implementation.

6.5.1 Dealing with uncertainty in the preparation of strategy statements

As mentioned in section 4.3, one way in which some departments and offices have dealt with the issue of ensuring their objectives and strategies stay relevant over the period of the strategy statement is to pitch them at a relatively high level, not necessarily related to day-to-day organisational activities and structures. This requires a delicate balancing out, in that if strategies and objectives are set at too high a level, they can become so general as to be meaningless.

More fundamental is the question of developing appropriate strategies to deal with uncertain futures. A recent review of strategic management initiatives in the civil service in several countries found that in Ireland techniques such as scenario planning were relatively little used compared to elsewhere (Green, 1998: p. 545). There is less questioning of the status quo and exploration of new ways of doing business in the future. Strategies outlined in strategy statements do not tend to deal with potential future change particularly well.

One academic study (Courtney et al, 1997) has indicated that there are four different levels of uncertainty facing strategic decision-makers:

- *Level 1 – clear enough future.* Here, managers can develop a single forecast of the future that is precise enough for strategy development.

- *Level 2 – alternative futures.* Here, the future can be described as one of a few alternative outcomes. Analysis cannot predict which outcome will occur, though it may help establish possibilities.

- *Level 3 – a range of futures.* Here, a range of possible futures can be identified, defined by a limited number of key variables. But the actual outcome may lie anywhere within this range.

- *Level 4 - true ambiguity.* Here multiple dimensions of uncertainty interact to create an environment that is virtually impossible to predict. These situations are relatively rare and tend to migrate to one of the other levels over time.

Level one situations tend to be the most addressed in strategy statements. However, it is at levels two and three that difficult strategic choices face government departments and offices. Techniques such as scenario planning, open simulation and game theory are needed here to facilitate thinking on how to address such issues (Joyce, 1999). While it is possible to over-hype the potential benefits of such techniques, scenario planning does offer a means of scanning the environment, not just for what is currently there, but for what could be (Cribb, 1998).

In terms of how departments and offices may position themselves to deal with alternative scenarios, Courtney et al (1997) suggest three possible strategic postures:

- *Shape the future.* Whereby the organisation plays a leadership role in devising a desired new direction with regard to a particular issue.

- *Adapt to the future.* Where strategies are reliant on the ability to recognise and respond quickly to environmental changes.

- *Reserve the right to play.* Where the future is seen as too uncertain to commit to a particular direction, and a watching brief is kept until the environment becomes less uncertain.

In general, the above would suggest that in the strategic management process more emphasis might be given to scenario development exercises (in other words a 'what-if' type of analysis). In particular, when carrying out environmental analysis, scenario development may play a useful role in some circumstances. While in some policy fields it will be possible to predict the future well enough to develop stable strategies, in others, levels of uncertainty will be such that a range of strategic options will be needed that can be developed into more detailed strategies at the appropriate time.

Some administrations are beginning to address this issue. In Australia, for example, a Futures Forum has been established, sponsored by the Public Service and Merit Protection Commission. This forum provides a network for managers in departments involved in the creation of strategy. The output of departmental scenario planning and other futures-related activities is shared and discussed, and lessons are learned regarding methodologies and impact. In the UK, the Performance and Innovation Unit based in the Cabinet Office is running a Strategic Challenges Project. This project aims to identify some of the key challenges that the UK government is likely to encounter over the next ten to fifteen years, particularly those with broad cross-departmental implications that are not currently on the agenda of individual government departments.

While these examples show what can be done, it is also important to recognise that there are limitations to futures planning. Not least of these is the time constraint on already hard-pressed managers and staff. It is important that a sense of perspective is maintained. For strategies which face particularly crucial and uncertain futures, a thorough scenario planning exercise may be warranted (how does the strategy operate under differing forecasts of economic growth, tax yields and so on). In other cases, a more rough and ready approach may serve. It is not suggested here that elaborate scenario development exercises become the routine for all strategies for all government departments and offices. The main concern is that the robustness of strategies is tested in some way to assess their merit under conditions of uncertainty.

6.5.2 Dealing with unplanned events when implementing strategy statements

Departments indicate that it is as part of the business planning process that unplanned and unexpected events are dealt with. Most annual business plans, as well as including activities clearly linked to objectives in the strategy statement, allow for the inclusion of new priority activities which may have arisen since the statement was produced. Also, fora for discussions on progress with regard to implementation of the business plan, such as the management advisory committee or divisional management meetings, are used to highlight new priorities. This will usually entail a reprioritisation of current activities. Departments and offices have found that having an explicit statement of proposed activities in the business plan can facilitate this discussion on reprioritisation, as it clarifies the implications of moving resources around to address new priorities. However, rigidities in organisation structure can still at times be a barrier to the reallocation of resources.

Sound monitoring and control systems are also needed to cope with unplanned events during implementation.

Good monitoring data provide management with early warning of new developments and provide a basis for any necessary corrective actions (Joyce, 1999). This underlines the importance of having sound management information systems to underpin goals, objectives and strategies.

6.6 Conclusions

The need for the strategy statement to link with other management processes is stressed in this chapter. These linkages are important if strategy statements are to have the desired impact. In particular, the need for strategy statements to inform and be informed by the business planning process is highlighted. It is through the business planning process that objectives and strategies are realised. Review and reporting mechanisms also have an important role to play in tracking progress, with the annual progress report as a potentially useful means of reporting on performance. Finally, the importance of developing process and procedures to deal with unplanned and unexpected events is highlighted. The impact of strategy statements will be limited if they are over-rigid and fail to identify or create means of responding to changing circumstances. Scenario planning, either formal or informal, can sometimes play a useful role in assessing the robustness of strategies to cope with changing circumstances.

PART 7

Conclusions and Recommendations

7.1 Introduction

A first point to be made concerns the evolving role of strategy statements. As noted in this study, the 1998 statements represent an improvement on the 1996 statements. This improvement covers both the content of the statements, in terms of the issues covered and how they are addressed, and the process of strategy formulation and implementation, notably the increasing involvement of staff through partnership arrangements and greater recognition of the need to align organisational structures and systems with strategic goals and objectives. As with any new major initiative, there is a learning curve to be gone through, and the signs are that learning is taking place and that strategy statements are becoming more central to the overall management of government departments and offices.

This is not to say, however, that the learning is complete. There is still significant room for improvement in both the process of producing and implementing strategy statements, and in their content. Some of the main limitations of current strategy statements were identified in Part 4 and are summarised in Table 7.1 There are also limitations with regard to the process and impact of strategy statement development and implementation. Many staff still have little engagement with, or sense of ownership of, the issues outlined in strategy statements.

Conclusions with regard to the main strengths and weaknesses of strategy statements are outlined below. These conclusions are put in the context of the role of strategy statements in the overall management of government departments and offices. Arising from these conclusions, recommendations are made aimed at enhancing the role of strategy statements in the future. The emphasis is on continuing the positive developments to date with regard to strategic management practice in the civil service.

Table 7.1: Limitations of Current Strategy Statements

- *Environmental analysis.* A tendency in some statements simply to list issues rather than explore possible scenarios and challenge the status quo. Often a weak linkage between the analysis and established objectives and strategies.

- *Identification of objectives, outputs and strategies.* Some confusion of terminology. Some goals and objectives not clearly focused on outcomes. Limited discussion of resource implications.

- *Assessment of customer/client interests and needs.* Little evidence of assessment of customer/client needs. Limited linkage between Customer Action Plans and objectives and strategies in some cases.

- *Cross-departmental and cross-functional issues.* A tendency to simply list issues rather than highlight what needs to be done, and how, to secure better co-ordination.

- *Performance measurement.* Lack of clarity with regard to many of the measures used, and only a limited range of activities covered by performance measures.

- *Embedding the strategic management process.* Activities outlined here are often not clearly linked to the environmental analysis and emergent strategies.

7.2 Conclusions: the role of strategy statements in the management of government departments and offices

In pulling together the findings from this study, the central role of the strategy statement in the management of departments and offices is apparent. Under the Public Service Management Act, 1997, there is a legal obligation for strategy statements to be produced, setting out the key objectives, outputs and related strategies of the department or office. The importance of ensuring that strategy statements link with other management processes such as business planning, review, and resource allocation has been highlighted in this study. It is through these linkages that strategy statements become an integral part of the strategic management process in departments and offices.

The key linkages for strategy statements, and the central role of strategy statements in the management process, are illustrated in Figure 7.1, which provides a

*Figure 7.1 The Central Role of Strategy Statements in the
Management of Government Departments and Offices*

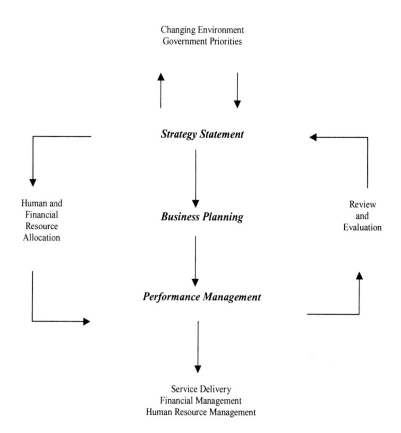

framework for drawing conclusions on the role of strategy
statements to date.   In particular, it can be seen that
strategy statements both influence and are influenced by
five main areas of management activity:

- *The   strategy   statement   and   the   changing
  environment/government priorities.* The need for
  statements at the political/administrative interface to
  reflect and influence environmental changes and key
  government priorities.

- *The strategy statement and human and financial resource allocation.* The linkages between objectives and strategies outlined in statements and human resource planning and allocation and budgetary decisions.

- *The strategy statement and business planning/ performance management.* The step down from strategies to detailed actions in business plans and performance management at team and individual level.

- *The strategy statement and review and evaluation.* The management of changing priorities and unplanned events, together with the review of progress with regard to strategy implementation.

- *The strategy statement and ultimate outcomes.* The impact of strategy statements on service delivery, and management of the human and financial resources in the civil service.

7.2.1   *The strategy statement and the changing environment/government priorities*

Environmental analysis is a central component of the strategic management process, providing the context for looking afresh at existing ways of doing things and identifying new issues.   In general, this task has been performed reasonably well to date, with improvement evident between 1996 and 1998.   One limitation with existing practice in some statements is a sense that environmental analysis is undertaken as an end in itself, rather than being clearly linked to the rest of the statement. A further limitation concerns the absence of scenario planning, open simulation or similar techniques for dealing with the issues of uncertain futures.

It is also at this level of the broader environment within which departments and offices operate that cross-departmental issues surface.   There has been an increasing recognition of the importance of cross-departmental issues, as illustrated by their more comprehensive coverage in 1998 compared to 1996 statements.   However, as with environmental analysis, there is sometimes a failure to move on from simply identifying issues and listing other departments or agencies involved. Departments need to be proactive in co-operating when addressing cross-departmental issues. In the UK, several cross-cutting issues have been taken away from departments who were seen as unable to make sufficient progress, and given to a central unit – the Performance and Innovation Unit – to secure active attention and co-operation (Boyle, 1999).

Changing government priorities are also a major influence on the continuing relevance of strategy statements. In general, the business planning process is seen as providing a suitable forum where such issues can be dealt with. Addressing government priorities also raises the broader issue of where strategy statements fit in the political/administrative interface. On the positive side, strategy statements are seen as helping clarify responsibility and accountability issues between ministers and secretaries general. However, while ministers have accepted strategy statements as part of the strategic management process, there is little evidence of more general political engagement with strategy statements. The degree of political 'buy-in' is important given the role of politicians in building momentum for and sustaining change in public service reform initiatives (OECD, 1999).

7.2.2   The strategy statement and human and financial resource allocation

The SMI guidelines highlight the need for strategy statements to pay attention to the alignment of a range of internal issues to ensure that the SMI process is embedded in the day-to-day work of a department, as opposed to simply being an 'add-on'. Part 3 indicates that key factors requiring such alignment are the allocation of both financial and human resources. The conclusions in relation to efforts made by departments to secure such alignment will now be considered.

Financial allocation

There must be clear links between the strategic planning

process and the allocation and spending of financial resources. Overall, the strategy statements do not adequately capture such linkages, although this does not necessarily imply that objectives and strategies are not costed or considered in the context of the estimates or budgetary process. At the same time, it could be argued that an explicit and visible linkage between desired objectives and their likely financial implications is useful for a number of reasons. Firstly, it can enhance the subsequent measurement of performance against objectives, since impact and outcomes can be better assessed in terms of their efficiency and effectiveness. Secondly, some of the interviewees suggest that a lack of focus on the financial implications of goals and objectives hampers the making of strategic choices, and that a more explicit focus on financial allocations might facilitate a greater prioritisation of or 'trade-off' among strategic choices.

Also, a clear aim of strategy statements is that they should represent the *collective* views of senior management as opposed to being 'sectionalised' statements. However, the findings suggest that while co-operation at senior management level is increasing, there is still a degree of competition for financial resources among divisions within departments, which undermines the achievement of a shared consensus on how financial resources might be best allocated to meet key strategic issues. To a large degree, this may be a reflection of existing structures, particularly where departments have multi-functional or multi-divisional objectives, which may result in an element of territorialism among divisions or functions. Clearly, there may be a need for greater cohesiveness and understanding among divisions to ensure that financial resources are allocated in a way that meets the collective views of senior management and best reflect the strategic priorities of a department.

Any consideration of financial resource allocation must take into account ongoing reforms in this area, which have the potential to strengthen the weaknesses identified in the foregoing paragraph. The development of multi-annual budgeting, for example, is seen as 'congruent with wider managerial changes in the civil service' (*Financial*

Management in a Reformed Public Service, 1999), including those arising under the Public Service Management Act, 1997, in which secretaries general have formal responsibility for the production of strategy statements and the day-to-day running of departments. Under the multi-annual budgeting system, it is anticipated that the provision of three-year resource allocations should encourage line departments to prioritise spending, focus on outcomes and outputs, and free up resources for service development. Similarly, proposals to introduce greater flexibility in the administrative budget system may enhance resource allocation within departments.

Human resource allocation
The findings suggest that securing the alignment of HR strategy with business strategy is one of the most difficult aspects of the strategy-making process. Very few departments have made attempts within their strategy statement to identify the HR implications of objectives and strategies. By implication, the setting of objectives and strategies may require a reallocation of human resources, yet the impression gained from many statements is that new objectives and strategies will simply 'fit' with the existing allocation of human resources. At the same time, it is important to recognise that the strategic alignment and allocation of human resources is constrained by certain structural features of the civil service. For example, human resource planning is influenced by a range of factors, including structural rigidity, a largely centralised recruitment and selection system, and internal turnover due to interdepartmental competitions, which can make it difficult to plan ahead in terms of available and appropriate human resources. In addition, as noted above, there can be structural rigidities within departments which result in an element of competition for resources, which in turn may undermine the optimal allocation of human resources to strategic priorities. Some departments are beginning to tackle such issues by more effective collegiate decision making at senior management level. Also, the findings suggest that a greater and more effective use of cross-

functional teams might address these issues to some extent.

In addition, it is important to recognise that departments can influence the allocation of resources through a number of HR policies, including training and development, and internal promotions systems. The findings suggest that little effort was made to place such policies at a strategic, focused level in the statements. For example, in many cases, no attempt was made to assess existing competencies or skills against desired objectives or outputs.

7.2.3 The strategy statement and business planning/ performance management

Operationally, the link from strategy statements to business planning to performance management is crucial to strategy implementation. From this study, it is clear that most departments and offices aim to ensure an explicit link between strategy statements and business plans. Business plans are expected to identify how activities contained in the plan link to the higher-level objectives and strategies contained in strategy statements (this does not rule out also including new activities arising from changes in circumstances since the strategy statement was published).

It is clearly vital that there is consistency between strategy statements and business plans. Two key factors in ensuring consistency are the use of terminology and resource allocation. With regard to the use of terminology, the study found some confusion in the interpretation of terms such as goals, objectives and strategies. With regard to resource allocation, the study illustrates that the more clearly strategy statements and business plans can identify the programme and administrative expenditure implications of activities or groups of activities, the more effective the link with the budgetary process. The study also shows that this is an area that needs considerable further work by departments and offices.

While a formal performance management system was not in operation in the period under scrutiny in this study, it will be a feature when developing future strategy statements.   Clearly the same principles of ensuring consistency between activities outlined in the strategy statement and business plan apply here at the level of teams and individuals.   It will be important that the activities identified in the performance management system are clearly linked with business plans and strategy statements.

7.2.4   The strategy statement and review and evaluation

Feedback is a vital element in the strategic management process.   Performance measurement, ongoing review and evaluation activities are all important issues. Performance measurement is identified in the study as the weakest aspect of strategy statements to date, though, as in other areas, there is a notable improvement from 1996 to 1998. Many items identified as performance indicators are, in fact, vague and ambiguous.   Also, many of the indicators developed focus on process issues such as timeliness rather than on the desired and intermediate outcomes, and customer/client interests.

With regard to ongoing review, most departments and offices have developed monthly reporting on progress with regard to strategy implementation at divisional level, linked to reviewing progress versus the business plan.   At senior management level, quarterly reporting is more common, together with periodic scrutinies of divisional progress by the management advisory committee.   This latter forum provides a useful means of critically reviewing progress and highlighting issues in need of attention.

The annual progress report on strategy statement implementation, required under the terms of the Public Service Management Act, 1997, is an important review and accountability mechanism. While the first annual progress reports in general present a positive picture of performance, they tend to give little sense of problems encountered or strategies not achieved. A more balanced view of progress would seem to be needed in annual progress reports.

Programme review and evaluation was only formally developed civil service wide in 1997, with the government's decision to introduce a programme of comprehensive expenditure reviews. Hence findings from reviews did not feature in the strategy statements reviewed. However, in future, programme reviews would be expected to feature in strategy statements; this occurs in the US, as exemplified in Annex 2, where evaluation is explicitly used in strategic plans to help in the development of goals, objectives and strategies.

7.2.5 The strategy statement and ultimate outcomes

Ultimately strategy statements will be judged on their ability to secure effective outputs in a range of areas which are critical to the success of the SMI programme of reform. In particular, the central thrust of *Delivering Better Government* (1996) is the achievement of excellent service to the public, and as a consequence the need for the development of a change programme which would result in a more efficient and effective civil service. As a consequence, there is a recognition of the need for a 'modernisation of personnel and financial management in the civil service' (p. 1). Thus the integration of strategy statements with business planning, aided by performance management, should result in improved service delivery, financial and human resource management. Although it is too early to assess the extent to which such outputs will be secured, it is possible to draw a number of conclusions from the research at this stage.

Service delivery

There is a range of measures which can be used to assess improvements in service delivery, including timeliness, quality of service, responsiveness, simplification of systems (see Humphreys et al, 1999, for a detailed consideration of this issue). While it is not possible to assess the extent to which strategy statements will play a role in achieving such impacts, it is possible to draw certain conclusions at this stage from the research undertaken. There is no doubt that departments have made greater efforts to focus on service delivery in their 1998 statements. However, the findings suggest that the improvement of service delivery is not yet a sufficiently central part of many of the statements. The implication of this is that the measurement of progress in relation to enhanced service delivery is made more difficult. On a positive note, the improvement of service delivery has recently been given renewed impetus with the setting up of a new Quality Customer Service Group.

Financial management
The development of effective financial management is necessary, if strategy statements are to play a central role in the management of departments. The report of the SMI Working Group on Financial Management, *Financial Management in a Reformed Public Service* (1999), indicates that existing financial management systems within government departments are more concerned with the control of inputs than with efficient and effective delivery of outputs, and it highlights the need for a more results-driven approach to financial management. In recognition of the need for an integration of financial management with the overall SMI process, a generic model is being developed by the Working Group, the implementation of which will involve a five-year programme of action to be managed by the Department of Finance. The aim of this is to facilitate more effective resource allocation, programme evaluation and managerial decision making.

Human resource management
There is a recognition within *Delivering Better Government* (1996) that the overall programme of change, in which strategy statements play a key role, must be supported by changes to existing structures and systems for HRM in the civil service. In order to develop a more proactive approach to HRM, the central HRM programme of change envisages a degree of decentralisation of HRM responsibilities to line departments, the devolution of responsibility for HRM to line managers and the professionalisation of the HR function. Most departments make reference to the changes proposed in their strategy statements, and many are also in

the process of developing high-level HR strategies. The interviews reveal that the development of a strategic approach to HRM is both the most critical and challenging issue that must be addressed if strategy statements are to be effectively implemented. Very little detail is provided within the statements as to how this will be addressed. Where HR issues are referred to they are generally unspecific. The implications of this are that the measurement of progress in relation to the alignment between HRM and strategy statements may not be adequately captured under the formal reporting process as set out in the Public Service Management Act, 1997, and this may dilute the strategic priority of this issue.

The role of partnership in progressing change in HRM policies was identified and stressed by most departments, although there is a recognition that the engagement of staff with management through partnership will require a different mindset to that typically found in traditional IR negotiations and structures.

Ultimately, what will be of interest is the extent to which there are clear links between HR strategies and strategy statements, since without such linkages it is very difficult to measure the contribution which HR strategy makes in securing the implementation of strategy statements. The implementation of the proposed new performance management system, which has the potential to facilitate the linking of individual performance and development plans with business plans, may remedy this to an extent in the next round of strategy statements.

7.3 Recommendations: enhancing the role of strategy statements

Drawing from the conclusions, and with an eye to the next and future rounds of strategy statement development, it is useful to highlight aspects of practice which can be developed to improve strategy statements in the future. In particular, issues are outlined here which could enhance the role of strategy statements at the strategy formulation stage, when determining the content of strategy statements, and at strategy implementation.

7.3.1 Strategy statement formulation

There are a number of issues which were highlighted in this study to which departments and offices should give attention in the process of formulating strategy:

- Strategy should be formulated to take account of the collective views of the organisation, in order to ensure greater ownership of the strategic management process. A range of mechanisms can be deployed to this end, including, for example, the use of cross-functional teams and task-based groups. At the same time, in order to ensure that strategies which are collectively formulated reflect the strategic concerns of an organisation, there is a need for the senior management team to provide direction and leadership to ensure that the statement retains an appropriate high-level strategic focus. There is also a need for the effective engagement of ministers and the political process more generally.

- With regard to the specific formulation of strategy statements, there are a number of issues which must be addressed. Firstly, efforts should be made to meaningfully engage staff in the formulation process. While temporary team-based approaches can be very useful in this regard, partnership can provide a more long-term and institutionalised means of engaging staff in the process. It should be recognised, however, that staff and management may need to be equipped with the necessary skills and competencies to engage in strategy formulation in a partnership or other collaborative forum. For example, while the SMI guidelines provide a structure within which strategy might be formulated, specific skills and competencies may need to be developed to ensure that activities such as environmental analysis are properly carried out.

- Strategic management often implies a trade-off among strategic choices. This suggests that the formulation of strategies should not simply be a listing of existing activities. Rather, it may require a challenging appraisal of existing activities and a prioritisation of strategic choices, since not all strategies may be financially or operationally feasible within available resources. This implies the need for a realistic assessment of available resources within the context of desired objectives, and as a consequence a reallocation of financial and human resources to what are identified as the most strategically important concerns.

7.3.2 Strategy statement content

Developments in strategy formulation along the lines outlined above will lead to improvements in the content of strategy statements. Indeed, all the content issues raised below require attention at the strategy formulation stage if strategy statements are to be an effective element of the strategic management process. In particular, there are a number of issues highlighted throughout the study to which departments and offices should give attention:

- Environmental analysis should more clearly be seen to link through to the resulting objectives and strategies, with the implications of the analysis clearly specified. More use should be made of techniques such as scenario planning to deal with uncertain futures. Whatever methods are used, from the more sophisticated to the more simple, it is important that the robustness of strategies is tested. It is particularly important that strategies key to departmental progress are seen to be capable of coping with a range of possible futures. Also, the findings from programme reviews and evaluations should be seen to feed into the environmental analysis.

- Goals, objectives and strategies should be clearly defined and specified, with goals and objectives focused on outcomes where possible. Where achievement of goals and objectives is outside the direct control of a department or office, intermediate objectives should be set. The resource implications regarding the achievement of goals and objectives should be addressed in general terms, particularly in the context of multi-annual budgeting. To facilitate a common understanding of terminology, it is recommended that the following definitions be adopted:

- Goals. Generally fairly broad statements of intent, outcome focused, covering a particular sector or sphere of activity.
- Objectives. More specific statements of intent which indicate how the goals are to be achieved. May be outcome or output focused, or both. Defined in such a way that they are capable of allowing subsequent assessment as to whether or not they have been achieved. May sometimes usefully be supplemented by specific targets.
- Strategies. Detailed actions to be pursued in order to achieve or to support the achievement of goals and objectives.
- Outputs. The goods or services produced as a result of pursuing the specified goals and objectives. May be either generic outputs for an office or section, or specific outputs arising out of objectives and strategies.

- Customer/client expectations and needs assessments should clearly be a major driver of issues covered in strategy statements (including internal customers). The linkages between the strategy statement and Customer Action Plans should be clear.

- In detailing cross-departmental issues and cross-functional linkages, statements should not simply list issues, but should identify the issues of concern, outline who is involved and highlight what needs to be done. Actions needed to secure and improve co-operation and co-ordination should be detailed where possible.

- The specification of performance measures in statements is a challenging task, but one which requires further action. Having goals, objectives and strategies which are focused on results and as specific as possible facilitates the development of performance measures. Measures should be developed for as wide a range of activities as possible, including the development of measures from a customer/client perspective.

- Statements should describe and acknowledge the role played by staff in the development of strategy statements. They should also clearly identify the organisational implications of embedding the strategic management process. Structural and organisation development changes needed to ensure that strategies are achieved should be identified and actions proposed in these areas as necessary.

7.3.3 Strategy implementation

A number of recurring themes can be identified from this research which require consideration if the implementation of strategy is to be effectively achieved.

- To ensure the effective implementation of strategy, there is a need to devise HR strategies to fit business strategy. Notwithstanding the many influences which impact on human resource planning in the civil service (for example, centralised recruitment and selection, interdepartmental mobility through promotion), policies should be developed in relation to promotion and training and development to ensure that the right competencies and resources are available to achieve business objectives.

- Strategy implementation implies change and, as a consequence, there is a need to plan and manage the change process effectively through the use of organisation development interventions such as partnership committees and team-based projects. As with any organisation development initiative, such interventions should be designed to challenge existing assumptions and patterns of behaviour in order to meaningfully engage staff in the achievement of cultural change and, as a consequence, in strategy.

- Many strategies require co-operation with other agencies if they are to be implemented effectively. Strategies which cut across organisations require human resource, cultural and structural issues to be addressed. Tensions and issues of territoriality need to be tackled as part of the implementation process. Improved communications between policy makers and service deliverers is particularly important in securing effective delivery of cross-cutting strategies.

- There should be clear links between strategy statements and business plans. Equally, business plans should be translated to individual level if the strategy statement is to inform the day-to-day work of individuals. The forthcoming implementation of a new performance management scheme should provide a mechanism by which individual objectives can be formally identified and integrated with other performance-related issues, including training and development plans and performance measurement.

- Apart from fulfilling formal reporting requirements under the Public Service Management Act, 1997, the annual progress report on implementation of the strategy statement should be actively used to promote change. For this to happen, the reports must clearly indicate both areas of progress and areas where problems have been encountered or targets not met. Independent auditing or review of annual progress reports may enhance their credibility. Mechanisms should also be put in place to provide for continuous reporting of divisional and individual progress against desired objectives.

- There should be a better integration and synchronisation between strategy implementation and performance and financial management systems. For example, the evaluation of efficiency and effectiveness of strategies and goals through programme reviews should be used to inform subsequent strategy formulation. Similarly, multi-annual budgeting and accruals-based accounting have the potential to facilitate a more strategic outlook in financial terms. Departments and offices should also ensure that activities such as business planning, review and annual reports, performance management and the estimates process are synchronised and work together rather than being treated as separate exercises which put a strain on resources.

7.4 Concluding remarks

Strategy statements are a positive feature of the public service landscape. Ireland, along with the US and New Zealand, is a pioneer in using legally mandated strategic plans as part of the strategic management of government activities.

It is important that strategy statements are seen as part of a *process* of strategic management. Statements on their own have limited value. They must be at the hub of a range of management activities, including business planning, performance management, budgetary allocation and human resource strategy.

But an emphasis on process alone is not enough. It is also important to emphasise *action*. Just as statements themselves are incomplete unless part of a wider strategic management process, similarly the process itself is of limited value unless it leads to the desired actions. Ultimate judgement on the benefits or otherwise of strategy statements will depend on how effectively the statements contribute to the three broad goals set for them at the start of the strategic management initiative: to contribute to national development; to lead to better service for the public; and to deliver more effective use of resources.

REFERENCES

An Action Programme for the Millennium (1997), Joint Publication by Fianna Fáil Republican Party and Progressive Democrats.

Beer, M., R. A. Eisenstat and B. Spector (1993), 'Why change programs don't produce change', in T. D. Jick (ed.), *Managing Change, Concepts and Casps*, Boston: Kirwin.

Boyle, R. (1999), *The Management of Cross-Cutting Issues*, Discussion Paper no. 8, Committee for Public Management Research, Dublin: Institute of Public Administration.

Boyle, R. (1997a), *Developing an Integrated Performance Measurement Framework for the Irish Civil Service*, Discussion Paper no. 3, Committee for Public Management Research, Dublin: Institute of Public Administration.

Boyle, R. (1997b), *Team Based Working*, Discussion Paper no. 4, Committee for Public Management Research, Dublin: Institute of Public Administration.

Boyle, R. (1996), *Measuring Civil Service Performance*, Dublin: Institute of Public Administration.

Bryant, S. (1997), 'Strategic management: developing and realising a strategic vision', *Public Management*, Oct, vol. 79, no. 10, pp. 28–32.

Bryson, J. M. and W. D. Roering (1989), 'Applying private sector strategic planning in the public sector', in J. M. Bryson and R. C. Einsweiler (eds.), *Strategic Planning – Threats and Opportunities for Planners*, Chicago: Hannos Press.

Clarke, M. and J. Stewart (1991), *Strategies for Success, Local Government Management Board*, Oxfordshire: Henley.

Coughlan, D. (1991), 'Understanding Organisational Change: Part 1 Principles of Change', *World of Irish Nursing*, July/August.

Courtney, H., J. Kirkland and P. Viguerie (1997), 'Strategy under uncertainty', *Harvard Business Review*, November–December, pp. 67–79.

Cribb, J. (1998), 'Hyped-up or helpful? Scenario planning and the public service', *Public Sector*, vol. 21, no.6, pp. 23–26.

Deal, T. and A. Kennedy (1982), *Corporate Culture: The Rights and Rituals of Corporate Life*, Penguin: Harmondsworth.

Delivering Better Government (1996), *Second Report to Government of the Co-ordinating Group of Secretaries*, Dublin: Stationery Office.

96

Department of Finance (1999), *Programme of Change in Financial Management in the Civil Service under the Strategic Management Initiative*, Dublin: Department of Finance Press Office.

Department of Finance (1994), *Framework for the development of a strategic management process in the civil service*, March.

Elcock, H. (1996), 'Strategic management', in D. Farnham and S. Horton (eds.), *Managing the New Public Services*, London: Macmillan.

Farnham, D. and S. Horton (1996), *Managing the New Public Services*, London: Macmillan.

Financial Management in a Reformed Public Service (1999), Report of the SMI Working Group on Financial Management to the SMI Implementation Group, Dublin: Dara Design on behalf of the Financial Management Working Group.

Fombrun, C., N. Tichy, and M. Devanna (1984), *Strategic Human Resource Management,* New York: Wiley.

Green, S. (1998), 'Strategic management initiatives in the civil service: a cross-cultural comparison', *International Journal of Public Sector Management*, vol. 11, no.7, pp. 536–52.

Gunnigle, P., N. Heraty and M. Morley (1997), *Personnel and Human Resource Management, Theory and Practice in Ireland*, Dublin: Gill and Macmillan.

Hardy, C. (1994), *Managing Strategic Action: Mobilising Change Concepts, Readings and Cases*, London: Sage.

Hay, M. and P. Williamson (1991), 'Strategic staircases: planning the capabilities required for success', *Long Range Planning*, vol. 24, no. 4, pp. 36–43.

HM Treasury (1991), *Strategic Planning and Control in Government Departments*, London: HM Treasury, August.

Humphreys, P. C. (1998), *Improving Public Service Delivery*, Discussion Paper no. 7, Committee for Public Management Research, Dublin: Institute of Public Administration.

Humphreys, P. C., S. Fleming and O. O'Donnell (1999), *Improving Public Service in Ireland: A Case Study Approach*, Discussion Paper no. 11, Committee for Public Management Research, Dublin: Institute of Public Administration.

Joyce, P. (1999), *Strategic Management for the Public Services*, Buckingham: Open University Press.

Keogan, J. F. and D. McKevitt (1999), 'Another set of strategy statements: what is the evidence on implementation', *Administration*, vol. 47, no. 1, pp. 3–25.

Lawton, A. and A. Rose (1994), *Organisation and Management in the Public Sector*, 2nd edition, London: Pitman.

Link (1998a), 'Implementation Group guidelines for the preparation of strategy statements under the Public Service Management Act, 1997', *Link* – the Newsletter of the Strategic Management Initiative, April.

Link (1998b), 'Implementation Group guidelines for the preparation of business plans – July 1998', *Link* – the Newsletter of the Strategic Management Initiative, November.

McKevitt, D. (1998), *Managing Core Public Services*, Oxford: Blackwell.

McKevitt, D. and J. F. Keogan (1997), 'Making sense of strategy statements: a user's guide', *Administration*, vol. 45, no. 3, pp. 3–25.

O'Brien, G. (1998), 'Business strategy and human resource management', in W. K. Roche, K. Monks and J. Walsh (eds.), *Human Resource Strategies, Policy and Practice in Ireland*, Dublin: Oak Tree Press.

OECD (1999), *Synthesis of Reform Experiences in Nine OECD Countries: Change Management, OECD Symposium on Government of the Future: Getting From Here to There*, 14 to 15 September, Paris: OECD (www.oecd.org/puma).

Partnership 2000 for Inclusion, Employment and Competitiveness (1996), Dublin: Stationery Office.

Peters, T. J. and R. H. Waterman (1982), *In Search of Excellence: Lessons from America's Best Run Companies*, New York: Harper and Row.

Poister, T. H. and G. D. Streib (1999), 'Strategic management in the public sector', *Public Productivity and Management Review*, Mar, vol. 22, no. 3, pp. 308–25.

Programme for Prosperity and Fairness (2000), Dublin: Stationery Office.

Quinn, R. (1997), Address by Ruairi Quinn, TD, Minister for Finance, at the press conference to announce the Public Service Management Bill, 6 March.

Rashford, N. S. and D. Coughlan (1994), *The Dynamics of Organization Levels, A Change Framework for Managers and Consultants*, Reading, Mass: Addison-Wesley.

Reynolds, A. (1994), 'Developing strategic management in the Irish public service', speech by An Taoiseach, Government Buildings, 22 February.

Simpson, D. G. (1998), 'Why strategic planning is a waste of time and what you can do about it', *Long Range Planning*, vol. 31, no. 3, pp. 476-480.

Smither, R. D., J. M. Houston and S. D. McIntire (1996), *Organisation Development: Strategies for Changing Environments*, New York: Harper Collins.

Stone, W. S. and G. George (1997), 'On the folly of rewarding A while hoping for B: measuring and rewarding agency performance in public sector strategy', *Public Productivity and Management Review*, vol. 20, no. 3, pp. 308–23.

Thompson, J. L. (1997), *Strategic Management: Awareness and Change*, London: International Thomson Business Press.

US Department of Education Strategic Plan, 1998–2002 (1997), Washington DC: Department of Education (www.ed.gov).

Vinzant, D. H. and J. C. Vinzant (1996), 'Strategy and organizational capacity: finding a fit', *Public Productivity and Management Review*, vol. 20, no. 2, pp. 139–57.

List of Strategy Statements Reviewed

1996

Department of Agriculture, Food and Forestry
Department of Arts, Culture and the Gaeltacht
Office of the Attorney General
Central Statistics Office
Civil Service Commission
Office of the Comptroller and Auditor General
Department of Defence and Defence Forces
Department of Education
Department of Enterprise and Employment
Department of the Environment
Department of Equality and Law Reform
Department of Finance
Department of Foreign Affairs
Department of Health
Office of the Houses of the Oireachtas
Department of Justice
Land Registry and Registry of Deeds
Department of the Marine
Office of the Ombudsman
The Ordnance Survey
Office of Public Works
Office of the Revenue Commissioners
Department of Social Welfare
The State Laboratory
Office of the Tánaiste
Department of the Taoiseach
Department of Tourism and Trade
Department of Transport, Energy and Communications
Valuation Office

1998

Department of Agriculture and Food**
Department of Arts, Heritage, Gaeltacht and the Islands
Office of the Attorney General*
Central Statistics Office
Civil Service Commission*
Office of the Comptroller and Auditor General*
Department of Defence and the Defence Forces
Department of Education and Science
Department of Enterprise, Trade and Employment
Department of the Environment and Local Government
Department of Finance
Department of Foreign Affairs
Department of Health and Children
Office of the Houses of the Oireachtas*
Department of Justice, Equality and Law Reform
Land Registry and Registry of Deeds*
Department of the Marine and Natural Resources
Office of the Ombudsman*
Ordnance Survey Ireland
Department of Public Enterprise
Office of Public Works
Office of the Revenue Commissioners*
Department of Social, Community and Family Affairs
The State Laboratory*
Department of the Taoiseach
Department of Tourism, Sport and Recreation
Valuation Office

---

*   These strategy statements were carried over from 1996, either as they
       were or with only minor amendments. It was agreed under guidelines
       issued to secretaries general and heads of offices that if they felt their
       existing statement addressed all the major issues, they would not
       have to publish a new statement. This applied primarily to smaller
       offices.

**   The Department of Agriculture and Food was renamed the
       Department of Agriculture, Food and Rural Development in
       September 1999.

Extract from *US Department of Education Strategic Plan, 1998 – 2000*

US Department of Education Strategic Plan 1998– 2002 September 1997

Goal 2: Build a solid foundation for learning for all children
In fostering the achievement of world-class student performance discussed in Goal 1, reform efforts need to focus on three main areas.

1. Promoting family and community efforts to support children's early development and education, to ensure that all children have an appropriate preparation for school.
2. Identifying what students will need to know and be able to do in core subject areas and what strategies are effective in improving instruction. Federal programs and efforts across the nation must focus on enabling all students to master fundamental and advanced reading and math skills. Children need to be able to read independently and effectively by the end of third grade, to be able to apply reading to learning other subjects.

    Similarly, acquiring mathematics skills and knowledge that prepare students for algebra, geometry, and more advanced work is critical to students success in high school and beyond. In mathematics, the latest results from the Third International Mathematics and Science Study affirm that poor US performance in the eighth grade is linked to mediocre content, lack of instructional rigor, and inadequate training and support for quality teaching.
3. Meeting the diverse needs of the student population, so that all students – including limited-English proficient students, students with disabilities, migrant students,

students in high-poverty schools, and any students at risk of not achieving the knowledge and skills required to achieve high state standards – receive the support and encouragement they need to succeed.

To address these three areas, the Department:

- Provides financial support to states and local school districts to help underwrite improvement.

- Will be offering voluntary, national tests in reading and math so that parents and communities will know how well their children and schools are performing in these two critical areas compared with those in other communities.

- Is implementing priority initiatives in reading and math to bring together resources throughout the Department as well as involve key partners in education and the business community in support.

- Promotes educational practices conducive to learning for all students.

- Eliminates discriminatory practices within schools that contribute to deficiencies in achievement.

Use of Evaluations and Assessments in Developing Goal 2
Goal 2 relies on having timely and accurate information with which to track the preparation of young children for school and the progress of all students in reaching challenging standards. Sources for this information include special analyses of the National Assessment of Educational Progress for high-poverty and Title I schools, and state and local assessments. The proposed national tests in reading and math will become a highly valuable source of information once they are implemented in states and communities.

- Cross-cutting evaluations of Goals 2000 and the reauthorized elementary and secondary programs are documenting how states and communities are implementing reforms to enable all students to achieve to challenging standards. Services provided to students who are the target populations for federal programs are a special focus. Studies have examined the supports that federal programs are providing to improve curriculum, technology, professional development and parental engagement.

- In the early implementation of the Even Start program, evaluation documented how more intensive programs – especially the parenting education component – were associated with strong program results for children. This and other findings helped to shape Even Start's reauthorization. Evaluations will continue to document how services affect children's school readiness and help parents support learning at home.

Objectives, Indicators and Strategies

Objective 2.1: All children enter school ready to learn.

Performance indicators:

1. *Kindergarten and first grade teachers will increasingly report that their students enter school ready to learn reading and math.*

2. *The disparity in preschool participation rates between children from high-income families and children from low-income families will decline year by year.*

3. *The percentage of children from birth to five years old whose parents read to them or tell them stories regularly will continually increase.*

Recent research has highlighted the importance of the earliest years of life for children's later success. Children's early learning experiences, or lack of them, have consequences that extend into the long term. Research on early brain development reveals that if some learning experiences are not introduced to children at an early age, the children will find learning more difficult later. Furthermore, children who enter school ready to learn are more likely to achieve to high standards than children who are inadequately prepared. High-quality preschool and child care are integral in preparing children adequately for school.

Core Strategies:

- Interagency coordination and services integration. Support children at risk of early school failure by coordinating with the Department of Health and Human Service's (HHS) Head Start program, HHS' and Department of Agriculture's nutrition support programs, and other federal programs and services for young children to ensure that their needs are met and to reduce the burden on families and schools of working with multiple providers.

- Financial support for children who are educationally disadvantaged or have disabilities. Provide resources to states and local school districts under Title I for preschool programs and Even Start, and to states and local providers under the Individuals with Disabilities Education Act (IDEA) for programs aimed at infants and toddlers and preschool children with disabilities or at risk of developing disabling conditions.

- Research, development, and technical assistance.
    - Identify, evaluate and encourage the use of programs for young children that make use of the latest research on early brain development, early intervention, and high-quality nurturing.
    - Develop, field test, and evaluate models of effective practice through such programs as Even Start that can be shared with local Head Start, Title I preschool, and IDEA preschool projects and with states, local districts, and community-based organizations.
    - Work with experts to develop an agreed-upon definition of school readiness and to establish a core set of standards that Even Start, Title I preschool and IDEA programs will use with preschoolers.

- Development and dissemination of easy-to-use kits for learning at home. Support family practices that encourage early learning by developing and disseminating educational materials for parents and their young children, such as the Ready*Set*Read Early Childhood Kit.

- Development of readiness indicators. Develop indicators of young children's knowledge and school readiness by working with HHS and other organizations, incorporating measures form the Early Childhood Longitudinal Study and other studies of children's school readiness.

* * *

Goal 4: Make ED a high-performance organization by focusing on results, service quality, and customer satisfaction

To help students reach challenging academic standards, to help build a solid foundation for learning for all students, and to ensure access to postsecondary education and lifelong learning, the Department must be committed to world-class management, quality service, and customer satisfaction. To be a leader in educational reforms, the Department has to be a leader in organizational and internal performance reforms. To achieve these results requires breakthrough thinking and accomplishments – in customer service, support for our partners, educational research, technology both internal and external, workforce planning and development, financial integrity, and strategic planning and performance measurement.

To become a high-performance organization, the Department must become 'results and accountability driven'. This will happen when we:

- Identify our customers and meet or surpass their needs

- Set goals and establish or improve our performance measurement systems to track progress

- Determine how best to work with our partners to reach program goals

- Continually seek new ways to provide services more efficiently and with higher quality

- Identify effective practices in education through R&D and evaluation, and get the information out to our customers and partners

During the past few years, we have made much progress in transforming ED into a high performance organisation. But more remains to be done. The objectives in Goal 4 and objective 3.3 in Goal 3 identify critical management processes for the Department that need ongoing attention or further development.

Use of Evaluations and Assessments in Developing Goal 4

- In its report *Department of Education: Long Standing Management Problems Hamper Reforms* (May 1993), the General Accounting Office (GAO) criticized the Department for not emphasizing good, sensible management techniques to accomplish its goals. This report further highlighted a lack of strategic planning, poor quality data, unqualified technical staff and a focus on short term fixes rather than long term solutions. This report, along with internal recognition of serious problems by new Administration officials, led to development of the Department's first strategic plan, establishment of standing committees for management reform, re-engineering of key processes including regulations and grants management, establishment of customer service standards and centralization of responses to customer inquiries, and other management reforms. Notwithstanding our having achieved significant improvements since that report, work is still needed in some of the areas it identified, including the need to improve the quality of performance data on our programs and operations.

- In 1993 and 1996, the Department surveyed all managers and staff on experiences and opinions about their work, working environment and support. The results of the employee surveys helped to set the direction for some of the objectives in Goal 4.

- To identify ways to improve customer service, we've followed Executive Order 12862, 'Setting Customer Service Standards', as well as used internal surveys of key offices and focus groups to establish strategies and measures for customer satisfaction. We tested telephone and employee responsiveness in a 'mystery shopper' survey. We also reviewed several GAO reports that offered suggestions for ways to improve our service to customers.

- When our office of research and statistics (Office of Educational Research and Improvement, or OERI) was scheduled for reauthorization, the National Academy of Sciences was asked to consider how federally-supported educational research could better contribute to improving the nation's education. The Academy, through its National Research Council, convened 15 distinguished experts to conduct the study. OERI adopted many of the report's recommendations, which also influenced selection of the strategies and indicators in this plan.

- To identify priorities for research, the Department conducted over 45 discussion groups to get input on national priorities for research in education. The resulting data and recommendations appear in the report *Building Knowledge for a Nation of Learners: A Framework for Education Research*, 1997.

- To help introduce management innovations, the Department's principal office components (POCs) have joined in partnership to do management reviews and make recommendations on areas that can be improved through process improvement or organizational development activities.

- For our information technology systems, a recent independent verification and validation study by KPMG Peat Marwick on the Department's network infrastructure and operations provided important improvement recommendations. The recommendations were used in developing strategies for objective 4.4 and are being followed now as we improve our information systems.

- GAO's 1997 report on *Challenges in Promoting Access and Excellence in Education* noted the importance of having a sound integrated information technology strategy to manage a portfolio of information systems. We have included an indicator on Information Technology Investment Review Board assessments of major systems to ensure that systems are mission-driven and consistent with our information technology architecture.

Objectives, Indicators, and Strategies

Objective 4.1: Our customers receive fast, seamless service and dissemination of high-quality information and products.

Performance Indicators:

1. *By 2001 at least 90% of customers, internal and external, will agree that ED products, services, and information, including those on the Department's web site, are of high quality, timely, and accessible.*
2. *Department employees and front-line service centers will meet or exceed the Department's customer service standards by 2000.*
3. *Quarterly evaluation reports for the 'One-Pubs' system, based on quality assurance surveillance, will indicate that high standards of performance are achieved for dissemination of ED's information products by 2000.*

People who need answers to their queries want help, not busy signals and unreturned phone messages. Customer service isn't just a slogan, it is a necessary focus of our organisation. We believe that customers should have seamless access to information and services and are striving to meet the standards we have set for customer service. (See the Department's customer service standards.) The Department has sought our feedback from customers to improve our programs and services; and this feedback has led to significant improvements in the way we do business.

Core Strategies:

- *Standards.* Set, meet, and exceed the Department's customer service standards, especially on the front line by providing employee training, regular feedback on performance, adequate resources, equipment and incentives.

- *Customer feedback.* Develop a comprehensive, reliable system for receiving and acting on customer feedback, including customer complaints.

- *One-stop shopping for customers.* Establish a 'One-Pubs' system that enables our customers to receive publications and other information products without having to track them down from several offices.

- *Public outreach.* Conduct outreach activities to increase awareness and support for the Secretary's priorities among key constituency groups and the general public, using regional meetings and events, teleconferences, newsletters, targeted mailings, national conferences, satellite town meetings, information services via the Internet, and contacts with state and local governments and other federal agencies.

- *Full access.* Ensure that customers with disabilities have access to Department services and information by expanding our TTY system capacity and establishing an alternate format center to provide both braille and audiotape.

- *Employee resources.* Provide ED employees with technology needed to respond effectively to customer requests.

Extract on Resource Implications from *US Department of Education Strategic Plan, 1998 – 2002*

	Program Funding		Staffing (estimated FTE usage)		Administration Funding	
	Budget Authority/ Student Loans ($000s)	Percent of Total	Number	Percent of Total	Salaries and Expenses ($000s)	Percent of Total
Estimated Distribution of Funding and Staffing Resources to Strategic Plan Goals, based on FY 1997 budget authority and estimated new student loans						
Goal 1 and Goal 2 *(Ed's K-12 education programs)*						
ED's K-12 programs	$16,383,088	24.6%	557	12.9%	$60,519	7.5%
Goal 3 *(postsecondary, vocational rehabilitation, and adult education)*						
Postsecondary, vocational rehabilitation, and adult education programs, and student loans	$49,924,792	74.8%	1,875	42.0%	$529,589	65.6%
Goal 4 *(research, leadership/oversight/operations)*						
Research	$427,451	0.6%	387	8.6%	$44,098	5.5%
Leadership/oversight/ operations	$0	–	947	21.2%	$118,414	14.7%
Civil Rights, direct support						
Office of Civil Rights, Title IV Training and Advisory Services, Women's Educational Equity	$9,334	0.0%	682	15.3%	$55,112	6.8%
Total resources	**$66,744,655**	**100.0%**	**4,448**	**100%**	**$807,732**	**100%**

Timetabling the linkages between Strategy Statements, Business Plans, Performance Management, HR Strategy and Financial Estimates – Department of Public Enterprise

	SMI	Business Plans	Performance Management	HR Strategy	Financial Estimates
January			Set Targets		
February					
March		End quarterly review Business Plans	End quarterly review Performance Management	End quarterly review HR Strategy	Revised estimates published by Department of Finance
April	Commence drafting SMI Progress Report				Mid-month multi-annual budget returns to issue to D/Finance
May	Annual Progress Report on 1998 Strategy Statement under Public Service Management Act (unpublished)				End multi-annual budgets/NPCs to be agreed
June	Taoiseach's meeting with Minister/ Management Committee on progress on SMI\n\nDepartmental Annual Report (to include progress report on Strategy Statement – see May) to be published	End quarterly review	End quarterly review	End quarterly review	Estimates circular to issue from D/Finance
July					
August					
September		End quarterly review	End quarterly review	End quarterly review	Management Committee to agree Estimates for Department
October					Estimates to be agreed with D/Finance
November					Abridged Estimates
December		Year end review of Business Plans and agreement on next year's plan	Year end review of Performance Management targets	Year end review of HR strategy	Budget Day

112

Research Report Series

1. *Partnership at the Organisation Level in the Public Service*, Richard Boyle, 1998